ISLAMIC STATE

IT'S HISTORY, IDEOLOGY & CHALLENGE

ISLAMIC STATE

IT'S HISTORY, IDEOLOGY & CHALLENGE

JOSEPH V. MICALLEF

ANTIOCH DOWNS PRESS
VANCOUVER, PORTLAND

First Printing, 2015

ISBN 978-0-9947571-2-8
Digital Edition: ISBN 978-1-58710-647-7

ANTIOCH DOWNS PRESS
Vancouver, Portland
www.AntiochDownsPress.com

Table of Contents

Introduction

The rise of the Islamic State (IS) has fundamentally altered the reality of the contemporary Middle East. Part radical jihadists and part revolutionary government, IS, in the space of eighteen months, has carved out a territorial domain comparable to that of Great Britain, with a population of over eight million people. Equally at home with cutting edge social media, while advocating a return to a more traditional Muslim society, it is rapidly transforming its domain into a twenty-first century reincarnation of a thirteenth century Islamic caliphate.

In the process IS has morphed into a political entity never before seen—a terrorist nation, complete with its own army, currency, and passports—committed to a revolutionary strategy of creating a new Islamic caliphate in the historic lands of the Muslim Arab Empires of the ninth to the thirteenth century. This new caliphate, stretching from the Iberian Peninsula to the Indian subcontinent, is but a first step toward its declared strategy of a worldwide conquest that will ultimately lead to the Islamization of the globe.

It has amassed billions of dollars in assets, what appears, at least on paper, to be a well-armed, formidable army. In the process, not only has it plunged both Syria and Iraq into civil war, but has made them the epicenter of a broader Sunni-Shia rivalry that threatens to plunge the Muslim world into a global conflict. Its unspeakable brutality, its genocidal policies, and its murderous record are unmatched by any regime since Pol Pot or Nazi Germany. Its rise has upended the traditional politics of the Middle East, creating tensions between long standing allies while making reluctant, if not surreptitious, allies of long standing rivals like the United States and Iran.

This collection of essays, most of which appeared in print during the winter of 2015, look at the origins of the Islamic State, its evolution from the jihadist group Tawhid and Jihad to, first, al-Qaeda in Iraq, then Islamic State in Iraq (ISI) followed by Islamic State in Iraq and al-Sham (ISIS), and finally Islamic State (IS).[1] We will also look at its strategy and tactics during the Syrian and then the Iraqi civil war, and the implications of its rise on the contemporary Middle East.

This is not a book in the conventional sense as much as an ongoing "work in progress." It is too early to write the definitive history of the Islamic State. There is little information available beyond what has been reported in the public media. Most intelligence agencies are still protecting their sources, both to maintain their relevancy, and also their safety. Interviews of individuals who have direct knowledge of events is often times impossible and, even when it is feasible, often times poses risks to both the interviewee and their interviewer. Moreover, the situation is sufficiently fluid and complex, that any "book" will quickly lose its relevancy. Instead it's my intention to keep updating this work as the situation in the Middle East develops and as new facts come to life. A separate chapter on the ideology of jihadism and Islamic State will be added at a later date.

Chapter 1

Abu Musab al-Zarqawi and the Origins of Islamic State

Zarqawi: The Shaping of a Jihadist

He was born, Ahmed Fadil Nazzal al-Khalayleh on October 30, 1966, in the Jordanian city of Zarqa. His family, part of the Palestinian diaspora, belonged to the Beni Hassan tribe. It was one of Jordan's biggest semi-nomadic tribes. Its historic territory had extended across western Jordan and into the West Bank and the Galilee. The Beni Hassan tribe numbers around 200,000 members, organized into twelve principal clans. Little is known about his early life other than his family was poor and that he was one of ten children. He grew up a delinquent; a high school dropout, and was arrested some 37 times by Jordanian police for a variety of offenses, from dealing drugs, muggings, robbery, and extortion to other "street crimes." As a teenager he was implicated in the burglary of the home of a relative that ultimately resulted in the death of an uncle. There was little in his youth that would have indicated he would mature into a feared jihadist.

During one of his stints in a Jordanian jail, Khalayleh became exposed to radical Islam. At some point in his early 20s, following his release from jail, he traveled to Amman, the Jordanian capital, and enrolled in a Salafist mosque. Not much is known about this period of his life. By the time he was 23, he had become a devout Muslim, thoroughly imbued with the Salafist outlook and philosophy of jihad. Later that year, in 1989, he traveled to Afghanistan to join the mujahedeen fighting against the Soviet Union. Arriving in Pakistan, he discovered there was little for him to do. The Soviets had already withdrawn from Afghanistan, although the civil war against the Najibullah government still continued. His devotion notwithstanding, he had no military experience or training, did not speak any of the local languages, and was of little use to the Afghan mujahedeen who were actually bearing the brunt of the fighting.[2]

It was during his "Afghan period," sometime around 1991, when he adopted the *nom de guerre*, Abu Musab al-Zarqawi. At one point he announced, although he never followed through, his intention to move on to Chechnya; then widely believed to be the next jihadist hotspot. He spent four years in Pakistan and Afghanistan. While he was there he first met Imam Abu Muhammad Asem al-Maqdisi. A fellow Jordanian, it is the assumed name of

Isam Mohammad Tahir al-Barqawi, a Salafist jihadi, Jordanian-Palestinian, writer. He quickly became Zarqawi's spiritual and ideological mentor. It's not entirely clear what else Zarqawi did during this time. He studied at various madrassas in Pakistan and possibly in Afghanistan as well. During this period he met Osama bin Laden. According to several eyewitnesses, the two seemed to develop an instant dislike for each other. He also became a correspondent for a small jihadist magazine, Al-Bonian al Marsous.

Maqdisi believes that democratic governments are attempting to replace Allah as the "supreme legislator," and that the acceptance of man-made laws was a form of apostasy. He was the first prominent Salafist scholar to publically brand the House of Saud as unbelievers. Maqdisi is widely considered the most influential living theorist of jihadi terrorism. The Combating Terrorism Center at the United States Military Academy at West Point described him as the "key contemporary ideologue in the Jihadi intellectual universe."[3] His website http://www.tawhed.ws is closely monitored by analysts and his sermons appear regularly on YouTube.

In 1993, along with Maqdisi, he returned to Jordan. Maqdisi had established a Salafist inspired paramilitary group called al-Tawhid, "Monotheism," which was committed to the overthrow of the Jordanian monarchy. The name was later changed to Bay'at al-Iman, "Oath of Allegiance to the Prayer Leader." During this period Zarqawi may have traveled to Europe to set up cells among Jordanian émigrés there. The group was planning a series of bombings against Jordanian government and western organizations in Amman, when Zarqawi was arrested for manufacturing and storing explosives in his home. Found guilty, he was subsequently convicted and sentenced, in 1996, to 15 years in Swaqa prison. Maqdisi was also arrested. Arab prisons, including Jordanian ones, are notorious for their use of torture and other ill treatment of prisoners. Under Maqdisi's tutelage, Zarqawi became further radicalized while in prison and emerged as a leader of the jihadists incarcerated there. He was also appointed the head of al-Tawhid; although some have argued this was more of a takeover than a succession.

In 1999, as part of a general amnesty issued by the new Jordanian King Abdullah II, his sentence was commuted and he was released from prison. Shortly after his release, he became involved in an attempt to blow up the Radisson Hotel in Amman—a hotel frequented by American and European tourists, and businessmen. In addition, Zarqawi also planned bomb attacks against a border crossing on the West Bank between Israel and Jordan, a Christian holy site on Mount Nebo, and a site on the Jordan River where John the Baptist is said to have baptized Jesus. The latter two sites where particularly popular among Christian pilgrims. When the plots were discovered Zarqawi fled to Peshawar in Pakistan. Six years later, in 2005, he was involved in the successful bombing of the same Radisson Hotel, plus the Grand Hyatt and Days Inn.

Eventually, Zarqawi made his way to Herat, in northwest Afghanistan close to the Iranian border, where he established a training camp for Jordanian jihadists. During his time, with funding of 200,000 dollars that he had obtained from bin Laden, he established a new jihadist group called Jund al-Sham (Soldiers of the Levant, JS). The group had about 150 members. The camp specialized in the manufacture of chemical weapons. It had been infiltrated by Jordanian intelligence, however, and little came of it, although some of its members were implicated in a bombing in 2005, in Doha Qatar. In September 2001, Zarqawi sent a cell of JS to Germany to organize attacks against Jewish and Israeli facilities; however, nothing came of this effort.

The Herat camp has at times been described as an al-Qaeda training facility, and it has also been suggested that during this time Zarqawi joined al-Qaeda and pledged allegiance to bin Laden. However, testimony from a number of inmates at the Guantanamo Detention Camp, who were in Afghanistan at the time, describe the relationship between bin Laden and Zarqawi as tense and that Zarqawi was intent on maintaining his independence from al-Qaeda.[4] The two men had very different views on the strategy of global jihad. Bin Laden was primarily focused on the United States and saw an Islamic takeover of Saudi Arabia as forming the core of a future Islamic caliphate. Zarqawi was more concerned with toppling the Jordanian monarchy and moving on to any other Muslim country whose government was vulnerable to an Islamic revolution.

Zarqawi returned to Jordan sometime during the early part of 2001. He was arrested by Jordanian police but then subsequently released. Little is known of his whereabouts except that he returned to Afghanistan later that year after the launch of the US led invasion. He suffered a cracked rib when a house at his training camp in Herat, damaged by a US missile strike, collapsed on him. In December 2001 he fled to Iran, along with many al-Qaeda members, where he received medical treatment in Mashhad.[5] During his stay in Iran, the Jordanian government attempted to extradite him, but the Iranian government refused to turn him over to Jordanian authorities.[6] Sometime in 2002, Zarqawi made his way from Iran into northern Iraq. Unbeknownst to the United States, the American enforced no-fly zone over northern Iraq, while protecting Iraqi Kurds from Saddam Hussein's retaliation, had also, inadvertently, created a safe haven there for radical jihadist groups.[7] In Iraqi Kurdistan he received shelter from the jihadist group Ansar al-Islam (Helpers of Islam). During his time in Afghanistan, and subsequently after he arrived in Iraq, Zarqawi organized Jam'at al-Tawhid wa'al-Jihad (Organization for Monotheism and Jihad, JTJ) and set up a new training camp and chemical weapons facility in Biyara near the Iranian border. The name was later shortened to Tawhid wa'al Jihad (Monotheism and Jihad, TJ) in 2003. Despite American suspicions that Saddam Hussein was supporting al-Qaeda and other jihadist groups, no evidence of such support was ever found. From his base in northern Iraq, Zarqawi launched a series of attacks against targets in his native Jordan.

In February 2002, Zarqawi was implicated in a plot to assassinate General Ali Bourjaq, head of the Anti-Terrorism Unit of the General Intelligence Department, the Jordanian Intelligence Agency. Bourjaq was unharmed but two bystanders were killed by the bomb blast. On October 28, 2002, JTJ was involved in carrying out the assassination of Laurence Foley outside of his home in Amman, Jordan. Foley was a senior American diplomat with the Agency of International Development. Zarqawi was subsequently tried in absentia in Jordan and was sentenced to death for his involvement in the assassination. Concurrently, in 2003, TJ launched a series of deadly bomb attacks in Casablanca, Morocco and Istanbul, Turkey. Zarqawi also planned to use ricin poison for additional attacks in Europe. It does not appear, however, that any such attacks were carried out.

Operation Iraqi Freedom:
The Beginning of the Iraqi Insurgency

In March 2003, an invasion force comprised primarily of American and British troops, invaded Iraq. Dubbed, Operation Iraqi Freedom, it lasted from March 19 to May 1. By April 9, in the space of 21 days, the government of Saddam Hussein was toppled and Baghdad was occupied. Combat operations were completed and formal resistance by the Iraqi Army ended three weeks later. According to British intelligence, Zarqawi had set up sleeper cells in Baghdad, prior to the start of the invasion, with the intention that these would be activated once the US occupation began.[8] The intention was to attack American targets with car bombs and other weapons. During the actual invasion, TJ took credit for over 700 killings, mostly of Iraqi citizens, from bombings—although the full extent of their involvement has never been documented.[9] It's likely that they took credit for attacks launched by other militant groups.

By June of 2003, a low level insurgency was underway in central and northern Iraq, especially in the region known as the Sunni Triangle and, in particular, in the cities of Baghdad, Fallujah, and Tikrit, and the regions that surrounded them. The original insurgency was fueled primarily by remnants of the Ba'athist regime, chiefly its security services, elements of the Ba'ath party leadership, and especially the Fedayeen Saddam militia.[10] The militia was a paramilitary organization loyal to the former Ba'athist government of Saddam Hussein. Its name meant Saddam's Men of Sacrifice. At its height the militia numbered between 30,000 and 40,000 members.

Uday Hussein had organized the Fedayeen in 1995. Recruits were typically young Sunni men living in central Iraq, the region most loyal to Hussein and the Ba'ath party. They were not part of Iraq's regular armed forces. The Fedayeen reported directly to the presidential palace. They received only rudimentary military training and, unlike the elite Republican Guard, lacked any heavy weapons. Although the positions were unpaid, members enjoyed a range of benefits and services. They were also given a free hand to extort and steal property from the Shia population.

During the invasion, Fedayeen forces put up a determined resistance. Entrenching themselves in the cities, they focused on guerilla attacks against rear supply convoys in an attempt to slow down the rapid advance of coalition forces. They also acted to intimidate the Shia population and dissuade them from rebelling against the central government while, at the same time, stiffening the resolve of the Iraqi Army to resist the invasion. After May 1, some of the Fedayeen joined various jihadist organizations that had sprung up in the Sunni Triangle, while other units continued to operate independently. Attacks took the form of small groups firing assault rifles and RPGs, as well as using basic forms of improvised explosive devices (IEDs), against US patrols and convoys. Given their poor training, their attacks were often ineffective and the militia's casualties were high. The last major attack by Fedayeen guerillas occurred on November 30, 2003, when a group of 100 Fedayeen wearing their trademark uniforms, attached a US military convoy traveling through the town of Samara. After the capture of Saddam Hussein on December 13, 2003, the bulk of the remaining Fedayeen either abandoned further fighting or joined one of the jihadist organizations. There were, however, subsequent attempts to create Ba'athist militant groups from former members.[11]

Over the course of the summer the tempo of the insurgency steadily mounted. There was an average of a dozen attacks per day resulting in approximately seven casualties and one death among coalition forces. In addition, as jihadist groups began to take a more prominent role in the insurgency, the number of suicide bombings began to increase. The Fedayeen did not engage in suicide bombings, that form of attack was characteristic of jihadists. The most spectacular attack was the August 19 truck bombing of the Canal Hotel. The hotel was the headquarters of the United Nations Assistance Mission in Iraq. The attack killed 22 people associated with the U.N. Mission, and unspecified other Iraqis, and wounded over 100. Among the dead was Sergio Vieira de Mello, the United Nation's Special Representative in Iraq. The attack was followed by a second bombing of the hotel a month later, which resulted in the withdrawal of the 600 UN staff members in Iraq.

On August 29, Zarqawi carried out a car bombing attack on the Shia Imam Ali Mosque in Najaf. The *shahid,* "martyr," who carried out the bombing, might have been Zarqawi's father-in-law.[12] The attack killed 95 people, including the Ayatollah Mohammed Baqir al-Hakim, crowded around the mosque for Friday prayers. The bombing of the Canal Hotel marked the beginning of the Zarqawi led Iraqi insurgency, even though TJ led attacks had started concurrently with the occupation of Baghdad. Even more significantly, the attack on the Imam Ali Mosque was the first time an important Shia landmark had been targeted, and represented the expansion of the insurgency to target the Shia population of Iraq and its institutions.

Over the autumn of 2003, the pace and intensity of insurgent attacks continued to increase. On October 27, a series of simultaneous suicide car bomb attacks targeted three Iraqi police stations and the International Red Cross. Thirty-five people were killed and two hundred and twenty wounded. During the Muslim holy month of Ramadan, attacks increased to over 50 a day, resulting in US casualties of 82 dead and 337 wounded. The US responded by deploying the air forces to hit suspected ambush sites and mortar emplacements. In addition, surveillance of major infiltration routes, ground patrols, and raids on suspected insurgents were stepped up.

Insurgent attacks by followers of Abu Musab al-Zarqawi steadily increased during 2004. A series of massive bombings killed hundreds of Iraqi civilians, police, and other security personnel, most of whom were Shia. This period saw the emergence of Tawhid wa'al-Jihad and Zarqawi as a major factor within the jihadist insurgency, and marked the transition of the insurgency from the old Ba'athist elements to jihadists. Composed both of foreign fighters and native Sunni Iraqis, these organizations had a militant Salafist agenda.

On March 2, 2004, Zarqawi staged a series of bomb attacks on Shiites that killed 185 civilians during the Ashura holidays. The bombings initiated a campaign of assassinations, kidnappings, and attacks against Shiite civilians.

A suicide attack against a Shiite mosque in July killed 98 people. Another bomb attack in August killed more than 100 Shiite civilians. On September 14, Zarqawi released an audiotape where he declared "total war" on Iraq's Shia. The declaration was an escalation of hostility from Shia's cooperating with US military forces to all Shia regardless of their political posture.

On April 6, 2004, Zarqawi posted a message to Iraqi Sunnis where he declared that the Shia were not true Muslims:

"They are the enemies; so beware of them. The curse of Allah be on them!" [Qur'an al-Munafiqoon (the Hypocrites) 63:4]... Ibn Taymiyyah was right in his description of these people when they repudiated the people of Islam. He said: This is why they cooperated with the infidels and the Tartars... They were the main cause of the invasion of Muslim countries by Genghis Khan...Some of them cooperated with the Tartars and Franks (European Crusaders)...some of them (Shiites) backed the Christians...They (Shiites) harbor more evil and rancor against Muslims, big and small, devout and non-devout, than anyone else...They enjoy repudiating and cursing Muslim leaders, especially the orthodox caliphs and the ulema (clerics). To them, anyone who does not believe in the infallible Imam (Al-Mahdi)—who incidentally does not exist—is a nonbeliever in God and the prophet... whenever Christians and infidels triumphed over, it was a day of jubilation... This is the end of what Shaykh-al-Islam Ibn Taymiyyah said about them. It is as if he is living among us today, an eyewitness of what is taking place, and saying...They always support infidels, including Jews and Christians. They help them in killing Muslims."[13]

Unlike the other jihadist groups operating in Iraq, Zarqawi's agenda extended to other countries in the region, especially to his native Jordan. During 2004, TJ also attempted to organize an attack against a NATO summit being held in Istanbul on June 28 and 29. Earlier, on April 26, the Jordanian government announced that they had seized a cache of approximately 20 tons of chemicals and explosives from a TJ safe house in Amman.[14] The chemicals included what Jordanian authorities described as "nerve gas" and "blistering agents." The chemicals and explosives were intended for use in attacks against the US embassy, the office of the Jordanian prime minister, and the headquarters of the General Intelligence Directorate. Also seized were three heavy trucks, identical to the ones used by the Iraqi military, with front mounted plows designed to crash through security barricades. To this day it is not clear what the source of the chemical weapons and explosives was.

Zarqawi's militant anti-Shi'ism and his steadily rising tempo of violence brought a rebuke from his former spiritual mentor Maqdisi. First, in June, on his website www.almaqdisi.com, and later in a number of different interviews with Arab media, he criticized Zarqawi's tactics on both political and spiritual grounds. He also wrote several articles, of which the most notable was "Al-Zarqawi" Support and Advice," where he admonished his former pupil for the use of suicide bombings, the targeting of Shia and Sunni moderates, his uncompromising hostility towards Shias, and his spectacle of beheadings. He also criticized Zarqawi for insisting on carrying out military operations in Jordan that would inevitably result in the destruction of his Salafist followers there. Other prominent Sunni jihadist groups in Iraq also criticized Zarqawi, noting that he lacked the religious qualifications to opine on Islamic law and that his actions "damage the image of the jihad" and "jeopardize the success of the resistance."

In the meantime, a Shia insurgency led by Muqtada al-Sadr and his Mahdi Army led to violent riots and, following a coordinated assault, the seizing of control of Najaf, Kufa, al-Kut, portions of Baghdad, and the key southern cities of Nasiriya, Amarah, and Basra. The Shia insurgency led to a widespread collapse of the nascent Iraqi security forces with many soldiers deserting or defecting to the Mahdi Army.

As 2004 progressed, the jihadist insurgency rapidly intensified. The incorporation of many Ba'athist officers into the ranks of the Jihadists significantly improved their tactics and sophistication. By the end of the spring the cities of Fallujah, Samarra, Baquba, and Ramadi were firmly under jihadist control. American patrols in the cities ceased and US military operations in the area were curtailed for fear that additional civilian casualties would only serve to further inflame the insurgency. During this period, coalition forces and the nascent Iraqi government focused primarily on dealing with the Sadr and the Shia insurgency in the south.

Al-Qaeda in Iraq:
The Internationalization of the Insurgency

Beginning in February 2004, in an attempt to position Tawhid wa'al-Jihad as the leader of the jihadist insurgents, Zarqawi had initiated negotiations with bin Laden to bring his organization into the al-Qaeda fold. In October 2004, after eight months of negotiations, Zarqawi formally swore loyalty to bin Laden and was in turn appointed bin Laden's deputy.[15] Concurrently, Zarqawi changed the name of Tawhid to "Tanzim Qaidat al-Jihad fi Bilad al-Rafidayn" (Organization of Jihad's Base in Mesopotamia) and was commonly referred to "al-Qaeda in Iraq" (AQI). In turn, al-Qaeda's leadership appointed Zarqawi, Emir of al-Qaeda in the Country of Two Rivers. The alliance made sense for both sides. For al-Qaeda, then on the run with much of its infrastructure and organization destroyed and its key leadership in hiding, the affiliation with Zarqawi gave it relevance on what was then the front line of the jihadist struggle. For Zarqawi it bestowed al-Qaeda prestige and access to its funding networks to his organization as well as enhancing his standing among the jihadist networks in Iraq.

From the very beginning there existed significant differences over strategy between al-Qaeda and Zarqawi. Bin Laden wanted to unite both Shia and Sunni in a war "against the global infidel alliance," while Zarqawi argued that the "near enemy," the apostate Shia and moderate Sunni, posed a bigger threat than the "far enemy," the United States and its allies.[16] For Zarqawi, his anti-Shia campaign fulfilled both the objective of jihadist/Salafist purity as well as the tactical objective of rendering Iraq ungovernable by the Shia dominated government.

Al-Qaeda had always possessed a noticeable anti-Shia bias. In 1988, bin Laden had personally led a group of Taliban fighters to Gilgit in Pakistan to suppress a Shia revolt, which resulted in the massacre of several hundred Shiite civilians. Even today, jihadist groups in Pakistan affiliated with al-Qaeda continue to target Shia groups there. Nonetheless, ever since the early 1990s, bin Laden had been urging cooperation between Shia and Sunni jihadists. The two groups had in fact, on many occasions, cooperated with one another. Both the Revolutionary Guard in Iran and Hezbollah in Lebanon had at times assisted al-Qaeda operatives. Many al-Qaeda militants, including bin Laden's son Saad, found safe passage, if not a safe harbor, in Iran following the US led invasion of Afghanistan.[17] Western intelligence agencies have long held that elements in the Iranian government and military had supplied arms and explosives to al-Qaeda operatives in the past. The issue of strategy towards the Shia was never resolved, although bin Laden, when announcing his alliance with Zarqawi on December 28, 2004, did sanction the killing of Iraqi security and military forces on the basis that they were apostate Muslims.

Over the fall of 2004, US military forces launched an offensive against jihadist positions in the principal cities of the Sunni Triangle. The offensive culminated in an assault on Fallujah, dubbed Operation Phantom Fury. By the end of the fighting, over 50 US marines had been killed and several hundred wounded. Between 3,000 and 4,000 jihadist insurgents had been killed, but probably twice that many had escaped and melted into the civilian population. Civilian casualties in Fallujah had been heavy. The dispersion of jihadists outside of the Sunni Triangle sparked a spate of violent attacks in Mosul and Baghdad, as well as throughout Babil province. By the end of the year, the US military claimed that it had killed or captured more than 15,000 jihadists while suffering 848 killed in action and another 9,034 wounded. In addition, there were thousands of Iraqi security forces and civilians killed, the latter both as a result of jihadists' attacks and American military operations.

2005 was bracketed by two Iraqi elections. On January 31, Iraqis went to the polls to elect a government to draft a permanent constitution. At the end of the year, on December 15, Iraqis again went to the polls—this time to elect the Iraqi parliament. Although, officially, no major Iraqi cities remained in the hands of jihadists, government control in the Sunni Triangle remained tenuous. This period was marked by steadily escalating violence. A massive campaign of assassinations and suicide bombings, chiefly against Iraqi Shia civilians, as well as Iraqi police and security officials, was launched in order to disrupt the election. For Zarqawi, the very idea of democracy was at the center of the battle. "Democracy is based on the right to choose your religion," and such a choice "was against the rule of God he declared."[18] Guerrilla attacks steadily increased during April. In May, with the announcement of a new, Shia dominated, Iraqi government, jihadists unleashed a major offensive. Again, this was targeted primarily against Iraqi Shias, and thousands of civilians were killed.

Military operations were taking place largely in al-Anbar province, the largest province of Iraq, and home to a majority of its Sunni citizens. These operations consisted of US military forces and Iraqi military and police. The latter were predominantly Shia, and were drawn from the south. Fallujah and Ramadi, both located in al-Anbar, remained the principal base of jihadists and were only nominally under the control of the central government in Baghdad. Within al-Anbar, the Sunni insurgency was increasingly dominated by and under the control of Zarqawi's al-Qaeda in Iraq. In the fall, a new round of massive suicide bombings was launched against Shia civilian targets, resulting in the death of thousands of Iraqi Shias.

In the meantime, Zarqawi also continued to operate in his native Jordan. On November 9, al-Qaeda in Iraq dispatched suicide bombers against three hotels in Amman: the Grand Hyatt, the Days Inn and the Radisson SAS Hotel. The latter was the same hotel that Zarqawi had targeted in 1999. The three hotels were often frequented by foreign diplomats and were popular among Western tourists. The attacks killed 60 people and injured another 115. Most of the victims were Jordanians. Also among the dead were a number of high ranking Palestinian officials. The attack brought widespread condemnation within the Muslim community. Thousands of Jordanians marched through the streets of Amman denouncing Zarqawi. Fifty-seven members of his family took out half-page ads in Jordan's three principal newspapers condemning the attack and publically severing their links with Zarqawi "until doomsday."[19]

Notwithstanding the alliance between Zarqawi and al-Qaeda, tensions between the two organizations remained high, and the substantial differences between the two groups over what strategy to follow in Iraq continued. On July 9, 2005, Ayman al-Zawahiri, then al-Qaeda's second in command, had sent a letter to Zarqawi urging him to refrain from attacks against Shia civilians. In the letter, Zawahiri outlined the salient points of al-Qaeda's perspective and strategy for the war in Iraq. The letter made six key points, most of which would later serve as a template for the Islamic State's strategy in Iraq and Syria.

According to the document released by the Director of National Intelligence, among the letter's highlights were discussions indicating:

- The centrality of the war in Iraq for the global jihad;
- Al-Qaeda's point of view, the war would not end with the American withdrawal;
- An acknowledgment of the appeal of democracy to the Iraqis;
- The recognition of the need for political action equal to military action;
- The need to maintain popular support among both Sunni and Shia, at least until jihadist rule has been established.
- Admission that more than half the struggle is taking place "in the battlefield of the media."[20]

Zarqawi ignored the letter. Instead, he moved to bring the principal jihadist organizations together as the Mujahedeen Shura Council under his leadership. The Council reaffirmed Zarqawi's anti-Shia agenda, declaring that its purpose was "to ward off the invading kafir [infidels] and their apostate [i.e., Shia] stooges."[21] The stage was now set for an all-out civil war.

Zarqawi was killed on June 7, 2006, when two laser-guided bombs demolished a "safe house," approximately five miles north of Baquba. According to US military sources, a joint British-American taskforce dubbed Task Force 145 (based at Balad Air Base, Camp Anaconda), halfway between Samara and Baghdad, had tracked Zarqawi to the meeting and had called in an air strike. Two US Air Force F-16Cs were dispatched and the lead plane dropped two 500-pound bombs, a laser guided GBU-12 (Paveway II) and a GPS guided GBU-38 (JDAM), on the building. Five people were killed, reportedly including one of his wives and one of his children, however this has never been confirmed. Zarqawi survived the attack and was captured by Iraqi ground forces and turned over to US troops, but died shortly afterwards from injuries sustained in the attack.

The US government subsequently distributed an image of Zarqawi's corpse. The photograph was described as "grisly" and in poor taste by critics and that it would "inadvertently create an iconic image of Zarqawi" as a jihadist martyr.[22] Its experience with Zarqawi's death was the principal reason why the US government did not release any pictures of Osama bin Laden's corpse when he was killed in 2011. Following the death of Zarqawi, US government sources confirmed that it had received significant help from Jordanian intelligence sources, including the location of the safe house. It also disclosed that it had been tipped off to Zarqawi's presence at the safe house from individuals in Zarqawi's own organization. It's not clear whether that information was in fact true or simply an attempt by US intelligence agencies to create dissension within AQI. In any case, the house had been under surveillance for six weeks by a unit of Task Force 145.[23] It is likely that Zarqawi's presence there would have been recognized, regardless of whether or not the US had received any additional tips.

Zarqawi was replaced by Abu Hamza al-Muhajer, also known as Abu Ayyub al-Masri, as head of AQI. He was subsequently killed in a firefight at his house near Tikrit on April 18, 2010. On October 15, 2006, AQI, and the various jihadist organizations that comprised the Mujahedeen Shura Council, announced the creation of the Dawlat al Iraq al-Islamiyah (Islamic State of Iraq, ISI). Originally led by Abu Omar al-Baghdadi, the Head of the MSC, ISI would morph into the Islamic State of Iraq and the Levant (al-Sham) or ISIS and eventually, in 2014 into simply Islamic State (IS). Al-Baghdadi was reported killed on April 18, 2010, although doubts remain as to whether he actually ever really existed.[24] He was replaced by Abu Bakr al-Baghdadi who remains "Caliph" of Islamic State.

Postscript: The Legacy of Zarqawi

Zarqawi's "strategy of insurgency" was to create a backdrop of violence that would make Iraq ungovernable. To achieve that objective he targeted the "foreign occupiers," the Baghdad government and, particularly, the police and military forces on which it relied to maintain public order and project its power and, significantly, the civilian Shia population. That strategy was, in turn, based on a number of key assumptions. First that US military forces, and those of the other members of the International Multinational Force, would be ill equipped to fight a protracted insurgency in an urban setting and that any attempt to do so would create a level of civilian casualties that would rebound in favor of the jihadists. Secondly, after centuries of ill treatment, a Shia-Sunni reconciliation would prove difficult and that the historic distrust between the two communities would remain high. Thirdly, that the Sunni community would accept the leadership of the jihadists over that of their traditional tribal leaders, either because they supported the jihadists or because they would be intimidated by them. He was fundamentally correct on the first two assumptions and, in part, at least in the beginning, on the third assumption also.

Unfortunately for Iraq's Sunnis, they managed to inhabit the one portion of Iraq that was largely devoid of mineral wealth. Had the Sunni Triangle possessed significant oil fields, then the Sunni community would have had a much stronger hand to play in their dealings with the Iraqi government. As it was, finding themselves increasingly marginalized by the Baghdad government, they relied, in part, on the "jihadist card" to ensure that they would have "chips" to play at the negotiating table. The weakness of that strategy was that the Sunni tribal leadership couldn't control the jihadists, much less turn them on and off as their success in negotiating with Baghdad required. Conversely, the jihadists depended, if not on the outward support of the Sunni community, at the very least on its acquiesce. Even one-way suicide missions still require a base of operations and some modicum of local support if they are to succeed.

The Sunni community in Iraq was not some hot bed of Wahhabi-like fundamentalism. It was not instinctively jihadist in temperament. Like neighboring Jordan and Syria, it may have been "culturally Islamic" and "Sunni oriented" but it was also a society that had secular and modernist elements. More importantly, its religious and ideological sentiments notwithstanding, like any community it was concerned with the more mundane but necessary aspects of modern life: employment, salaries, basic government services, utilities and infrastructure, and above all an environment where domestic life could function. At this point in the insurgency the jihadists could not supply any of these things.

We tend to see jihadism through the prism of ideology and religious beliefs. Jihadists are after all "holy warriors," devoted to their beliefs however misguided, destructive, or antiquated we might find them. Strange as it may seem however, jihadists often find themselves constrained by the same market and economic forces we associate with contemporary economic life. Jihadist organizations compete with one another for financial and political support. Money makes the jihadist's world go round just like it does that of their less ideological brethren. Money is what buys arms, pays salaries to militant troops, and allows the creation of organizational structures. Capital is required for growth—whether in a business enterprise or in a transnational jihadist organization.

Concepts like "market share" or "market leader" are not concepts that we typically associate with jihadists or terrorists, but in fact jihadist organizations compete with one another for "market share" and visibility just as surely as any consumer products company.[25] In that sense Zarqawi was the most "entrepreneurial" of the jihadists. At the height of the Iraqi insurgency, Zarqawi and his followers would often boast on their website and in their communications, that Tawhid was responsible for the majority of the car bombings and for the casualties among American and Iraqi soldiers. It was Zarqawi who launched the terrorist campaign against Shia civilians, who first targeted Shia holy sites, and who claimed responsibility for the overwhelming majority of Shia civilian casualties. In doing so he was successful in establishing himself as the face of the Iraqi insurgency and in parlaying that into greater financial and military support.

The prize for being the "market leader" was the recognition from al-Qaeda, then the premier and most "prestigious" transnational jihadist organization, of Tawhid as al-Qaeda's spear-carrier in Iraq. Zarqawi and bin Laden may have had little in common, they may have detested each other personally, but Tawhid, by virtue of its visibility in the Iraq insurgency, gave al-Qaeda something that it no longer had in 2004, geopolitical and ideological relevance on the front line of the jihadist struggle. In turn, by positioning itself as al-Qaeda's arm in Iraq, or Mesopotamia to use their vernacular, Zarqawi gained access to the prestige and more importantly the funding networks that bin Laden had at his disposal. Tactically and ideologically, there was a sharp difference between the two organizations, differences that were never reconciled. Al-Qaeda tried to rein in Zarqawi's radical anti-Shi'ism, but in the end it was Zarqawi's ideology that prevailed. The alliance would prove short lived and in the end the heir of Tawhid, Islamic State, would go on to supplant al-Qaeda as the preeminent transnational jihadist organization in the world. In the process, it would also, for the first time, make virulent anti-Shi'ism a central element of its jihadist struggle.

Chapter 2

Civil War and Its Aftermath 2006-2011

The Formation of the Mujahedeen Shura Council

On January 15, 2006, Abu Maysarah al-Iraqi, a spokesman for al-Qaeda in Iraq, announced on the jihadist website Hanin net the formation of the Majlis Shura a-'Mujahedeen fi al-Iraq (Mujahedeen Shura Council of Iraq, MSC).[26] The Council was an umbrella organization formed by a number of extremist jihadist groups in Iraq. The initial group consisted of six organizations: al-Qaeda in Iraq (AQI), Jaish al-Taiifa al-Mansoura (Army of the Victorious Sect), al-Awhal Brigades (Calamities or Horror Brigades), Saraya al-Jihad al-Islam (Islamic Jihad Brigades), al-Ghuraba Brigades (Foreigners Brigades), and Saraya Ansar al-Tawhid (the Monotheism Supporters Brigades). A seventh group, Jaish al-Sunnah wal Jama'a (Army of Adherents to the Sunna and the Community or Army of the Sunni Community), asked to join the group and publically called for other jihadist groups to join as well. At the time, US forces were tracking over eighty jihadist organizations operating in Iraq.

The emergence of the MSC has been variously interpreted as a consolidation of Zarqawi's position as leader of the jihadist movement in Iraq as well as an attempt by al-Qaeda to reduce Zarqawi's prominence by merging al-Qaeda in Iraq into a larger organization with new leadership. Neither interpretation is entirely correct, but both have some elements of truth to them. First of all, the MSC was not a creation of Zarqawi. Little is known about the organization prior to January 2006, but it appears that it had been in existence at least since 2005, and probably even sooner. Earlier, on May 2, 2005, in a statement to al Jazeera, the MSC had taken responsibility for the abduction of Douglas Wood, an Australian working in Iraq. Iraqi and US forces subsequently rescued him on June 15. The name Mujahedeen Shura Council had first appeared during the war in Chechnya a decade before, although it did not appear there were any specific links between the two organizations.

The MSC reiterated Zarqawi's position that the purpose of the council was to manage, "...the struggle in the battle of confrontation to ward off the invading kafir [infidels] and their apostate stooges...Uniting the word of the mujahedeen and closing their tranks...[and] determining a clear position toward developments and incidents so that people can see things clearly and the truth will not be confused with falsehood."[27]

The MSC continued Zarqawi's strategy of targeting Shia civilians. That strategy continued even after Zarqawi's death on June 7, 2006. In July 2006, over 1,600 Shia civilians were killed in attacks orchestrated by the MSC.

Zarqawi himself seemed to acknowledge his apparent demotion. In a communiqué issued in early 2006, he claimed that he "was honored to be a member of this blessed council with its wise leadership." Officially, the head of the MSC was Abdullah bin Rashid al-Baghdadi. He was identified as the *nom de guerre* of Hamid Dawud Mohamed Khalil al Zawi. However, this was never proven and US Forces subsequently concluded that Baghdadi never really existed.[28] In July 2007, a senior operative of al-Qaeda named Khaled al-Mashhadani, who had been captured by US military forces on July 2, 2007, claimed that Baghdadi was a fictional character created by al-Qaeda to put an Iraqi face on the jihadist movement in Iraq and to put some distance between Zarqawi's atrocities and al-Qaeda.[29] The same claim was echoed by Hamas in Iraq, another jihadist organization, in March 2008.

The use of the terms *majalis* and *shura* in the MSC's official name were intended to invoke the nomenclature of Arab government. *Majalis* is an Arabic term meaning "place of sitting" and is used to designate parliaments in a number of Arab countries in North Africa and the Middle East. *Shura* refers to a "consultative council." Such councils form an integral part of Arab governance. The Upper Chamber of Egypt's Parliament is called the Shura Council. In Saudi Arabia, a "Shura Council," the Consultative Assembly of Saudi Arabia, made up of 150 advisors, advises the king. The attempt to invoke the symbolism of governance was consistent with the advice of Ayman al-Zawahiri's July 9, 2005 letter to Zarqawi in which he stressed "the need for political action equal to military action."

The emergence of the MSC was a response both to the organization of an Iraqi government in Baghdad and to the emergence of a Sunni tribal chief led opposition, in Anbar province, to al-Qaeda in Iraq. The catalyst of what came to be called the Awakening Movement was a territorial dispute between the Albu Mahals tribe and the, al-Qaeda in Iraq supported, Al Salmani tribe. The leader of the Albu Mahals tribe, Sheik Abdul Sattar Buzaigh al-Rishawi, who had already lost his father and three brothers to AQI jihadists, proposed an alliance with a local US Marine Corp battalion. This was not the first time such a proposal had been made. Moreover, Sunni opposition to AQI and other jihadist groups in Anbar province had been building steadily over the previous two years. With the approval of the US government, the Marines began to supply weapons and training to the Sheik's men. In September 2006, Sheik al-Rishawi formed the Anbar Awakening Council to oppose the presence of foreign jihadists in Iraq.

A year later, on September 13, 2007, al-Rishawi was assassinated, along with two of his bodyguards, by a roadside bomb near his home in Ramadi.

The Origins of the Anbar Awakening Councils

The Anbar Awakening Councils was not the first attempt by Sunni tribal leaders in Anbar province to organize a regional government and attempt to restore order in the province following the fall of the Hussein government in Baghdad. In the summer of 2003, Sunni Sheiks in Anbar province led by Sheik Mudher al-Kharbit, paramount chief of the Dulaim tribe and Sheik Naeem al-Gaoud of the Al-Bu Nimr tribe, which are also part of the larger Dulaim tribe, and members of the former Hussein government agreed to select General Abdul Karim Burjis Arrawi, a former Baathist, as Governor of Anbar province. Coalition forces accepted the appointment of Burjis as acting governor, notwithstanding his ties to the previous Ba'athist government. He stepped down in July 2004 when three of his sons were kidnapped in Ramadi by al-Qaeda in Iraq. His resignation was one of the conditions demanded by AQI for their release. AQI subsequently released a video of Burjis announcing his resignation and apologizing for opposing AQI and the jihadist insurgency as well as for cooperating with coalition forces.

The Dulaim tribe consists of more than 1,000 clans and stretches across Anbar province into Jordan, eastern Syria and northern Kuwait. It numbers approximately seven million individuals, one of the largest of the Arab tribes, of which between two and three million reside in Iraq, mostly in Anbar province. The tribe is predominantly Sunni, although there is a handful of Shia clans as well. Historically, its hereditary leaders have come from the Albu Assaf clan. The Dulaim had a long history of insurgency against both the Ottoman Empire and later against the British colonial administration. Their relationship with Saddam Hussein and his Ba'athist government was complicated. The tribe made up over 10 percent of the Iraqi Army and over 20 percent of the elite Republican Guard units. On the other hand, the leadership of the Dulaim, primarily Sheik Mudher al-Kharbit and his brother Sheik Malik al-Kharbit, had long had a covert relationship with US intelligence agencies and had, on a number of occasions, discussed plans to stage a coup and topple Hussein. There were also reports that in the period prior to the invasion, the al-Kharbits had used their widespread commercial interests in Anbar to provide cover for CIA agents operating in the province.[30]

In March of 2005, a group of 50 sheiks in Anbar province met with Colonel Joseph Dunford, then Chief of Staff of the 1st Marine Division and asked that the U.S arm Sunni militias in order to resist AQI. The US government refused the request to arm Sunni militias and directed the sheiks to send their men to the Iraqi Army. At the same time a separate group, the Anbar People's Congress (APC), a coalition of Anbar tribal leaders based in Amman, Jordan, led by Talal al-Gaoud, patriarch of the al-Gaoud family of the Nimr tribe, was negotiating with American military representatives on a similar request. Representatives of the American military had been meeting with al-Gaoud and representatives of the APC since before the invasion of Iraqi. In late 2005 Sunni tribal leaders, led by Sheik Walid Abd al-Karim Mukhlif Fahadawi the paramount sheik of the Albu Fahad, again attempted to form an organization to counter AQI and other foreign jihadists in Anbar province by organizing the Anbar People's Committee. Fahadawi was subsequently kidnapped by AQI jihadists, dressed as Iraqi policemen, and murdered. After the subsequent assassinations of a number of other APC leaders, the organization disbanded.

In the meantime, Sunni organized vigilante justice against AQI and other jihadist groups began to increase. Such actions had started in 2004, and had steadily gained traction. The most prominent group was Farsan al-Rafidayn (the Knights of the Two Rivers) organized by a former Iraqi military officer named Saad al-Obaidi Ghaffoori under the pseudonym "Abu Abed." Organized in the Ameriyah neighborhood of Baghdad, a predominantly Sunni, wealthy district, in western Baghdad, the Knights of the Two Rivers cooperated with coalition forces to oust jihadist insurgents from the area.[31] In March 2005, in Ramadi, seven AQI jihadists were killed by members of the Dulaim tribe in retaliation for the murder of a clan leader, Lt. Colonel Sulaiman Ahmed Dulaim, and his three bodyguards on October 2, 2004. He was the Iraqi National Guard commander in Fallujah and Ramadi. Dulaim had been abducted and subsequently tortured before being shot.

After the assassination of Sheik Fahadawi, members of the Albu Fahad and Albu Bali clans formed an anti-AQI group known as Thwar al-Anbar (the Anbar Revolutionaries). The group never amounted to more than 30 members but it had a significant impact in the fight against AQI and many of its members would go to play a significant role in the Awakening Councils and the Sahwah al-Anbar (SAA) (Anbar Militias). The group was responsible for the killing of several AQI provincial emirs and their campaign acted as a lightning rod for the growing hostility towards AQI in Ramadi and Fallujah. The success of the Knights and their willingness to collaborate with US forces, as well as the emergence of groups like the Anbar Revolutionaries, coupled with the inability of US and Iraqi forces to pacify Anbar province, led the US government to support the organization and arming of the Sunni militias. The Knights of the Two Rivers, an obvious play on AQI's name of "al-Qaeda in the Country of Two Rivers," became the template for the Sunni militias of the Awakening Councils organized in Anbar, Salaheddin, Diyala, Nineveh, and Tamin provinces.

On September 11, 2006, the *Washington Post* published an article headlined "Situation Called Critical in Western Iraq." The article was largely based on a classified report, "State of the Insurgency in al-Anbar," which had been prepared by Colonel Peter Devlin, Chief of Intelligence for the US Marine Corp in Iraq, delivered to the Joint Chiefs of Staff. In his report, Devlin concluded that, "*MNF and ISF are no longer capable of militarily defeating the insurgency in al-Anbar and that AQI had become an integral part of the social fabric of western Iraq.*" He went on to add that AQI had "*eliminated, subsumed, marginalized, or co-opted*" all other jihadist insurgents, Sunni tribes, and political institutions in Anbar. The Marines he noted had managed to "*prevent things from getting far worse,*" and he recommended that the only way to reestablish control of the province was by "*organizing a sizeable and legally approved paramilitary force* or *by deploying an additional division in Anbar coupled with billions of dollars of aid.*" [32]

The Struggle for Anbar Province

The Anbar Awakening Council would be the third, and this time successful, attempt to organize a Sunni opposition to the jihadist insurgents in Anbar province and in the other Sunni dominated areas. They would be known by a variety of names: Abna al-Iraq (Sons of Iraq), Inqadh al-Anbar (Anbar Salvation), al-Majlis al-Watani li-Inqadh al-Iraq (National Council for the Salvation of Iraq), the Harakat a-Inqadh al-Sunni (Sunni Salvation Movement), among others. These "Concerned Local Citizens Committees," as the US military world refer to them, represented both the establishment of a local and provincial government and the organization of a Sunni militia force, "Sahwa," under the authority of the respective local sheiks.

The militias were funded directly by the US military at a cost of roughly sixteen million dollars a month. At their peak they numbered some 100,000 men. Many of the militia members were reportedly former insurgents and many had originally been sympathetic to the various jihadist groups. Their role was to patrol their local neighborhoods, cooperate with coalition forces in fighting Jihadist insurgents, and especially assist the US military to specifically target al-Qaeda in Iraq and minimize civilian casualties. While the growing rejection of the Al-Qaeda sponsored indiscriminate violence, the increasing association of Jihadism with "foreign fighters" and their practice of terrorizing Sunnis played a role in the formation of the Awakening Councils, ideology alone was not the only factor. The prospect of steady employment for Sunnis that had been marginalized both politically and economically by the fall of the Sunni-Ba'athist regime was equally, and perhaps more, important.

The growth of the Anbar Awakening Council and its associated militia coincided with the US military "surge" announced by President Bush on January 10, 2007. The dispatch of an additional 20,000 America troops, later increased to 30,000, precipitated vocal opposition in the US Congress. Several months later, Secretary of Defense, Robert Gates, announced that the tours of duty of American serviceman in Iraq and Afghanistan were being unilaterally extended to 16 months from 12 in a further, *de facto* escalation of American troop strength. At the same time, the Iraqi government, in an attempt to foster national unification as well as woo former Ba'athist supporters away from the jihadist groups, passed a law allowing former members of the Ba'ath Party to assume positions in the military, civil service, and in the government. The new law offered Ba'ath party members amnesty as well as the reinstatement of government pensions.

The combination of the Awakening Councils, the formation of a one hundred thousand plus Sunni militia force, the "surge" of American troops, and better tactics in urban warfare by coalition forces combined to steadily degrade AQI and other jihadist groups. Beginning in 2007, coalition forces and Sunni militias retook control of Ramadi followed by Hit, Haditha, and Rutbah and the balance of western Anbar province. In June 2007, US forces secured Fallujah, al-Karmah, and key portions of eastern Anbar province. Roughly two-thirds of Anbar's population lived in Fallujah and Ramadi. By September 2007, military operations against AQI and other jihadist groups had ended, with Anbar province and the rest of the notorious "Sunni Triangle of Death" under the control of the local Awakening Councils and American military forces. A year later, on September 1, 2009, the US military transferred political control of Anbar province to the Iraqi government in Baghdad. Military control was transferred to the Iraqi military on June 30, 2009, following the withdrawal of American combat troops from Iraqi towns and cities. US Marine forces in the province were replaced by US Army troops in January 2010. All combat troops were withdrawn during August

2010. The 4th Stryker Brigade, 2nd Infantry Division was the last combat brigade withdrawn from Iraq, on August 18. US troops continued in an advisory and support role, and continued to remain embedded in Iraqi units in Anbar until December 7, 2011.

The Iraqi government had initially been unsupportive of the Sunni militias, fearing that they would become the nucleus of "an armed Sunni opposition in the making" and be a "third military organization."[33] Baghdad wanted the Sunni militias under the direct command of the Iraqi military and police forces. There was also the fear that a civil war might erupt between rival Shia and Sunni militias. Between 2004 and 2008, Baghdad had been forced to deal with an ongoing Shia insurgency carried out by the Mahdi Army of Shia cleric Muqtada al-Sadr. The Iraqi's had done poorly at first against the Shia militias, with many ISF soldiers either abandoning their positions or defecting to the militias. The possibility of having to deal simultaneously with both a Shia and Sunni militia, much less the possibility of finding itself in the middle of a civil war between the two groups, was considered a serious threat by the Iraqi government of Prime Minister Nuri Kamal al-Maliki. Baghdad eventually relented its opposition to the Sunni militias and, under US pressure, agreed that the Sunni militias would eventually be absorbed into the Iraqi military and police forces.

The Iraqi government was quick to begin dismantling the Sunni militias and to cut back on their funding when their supervision was turned over to Baghdad by US military forces in October 2008. Notwithstanding Maliki's pledge to incorporate the 100,000 members of the Sunni militias into the Iraqi military and police forces, only about 17,000 were actually given permanent jobs. The balance, some 83,000 men, soon found themselves without employment or any prospect of one with an Iraqi government seemingly oblivious to the fact that their participation in the Awakening Movement now made them prime targets for jihadi violence. The Iraqi government has claimed that some 70,000 members of the Sunni militias were absorbed into the Iraqi Army and that another 30,000 to 40,000 are employed by the military and police forces to man checkpoints in Sunni areas. Sunni leaders dispute this claim, however, and claim that many of the Sunni militia has not been paid regularly and that the promised integration has never occurred.[34]

Moreover, in March 2009, Adel al-Mashhadani, the leader of the Awakening Council in Fadhil, a suburb of Baghdad, was arrested by Iraqi police on charges of murder, extortion, and violating the constitution, and of being the local leader of the Ba'ath Party's military wing. Two years later, on December 19, 2011, less than a week after US forces departed from Iraq, Maliki orchestrated the issue of a warrant against Tareq al-Hashimi, a Sunni and vice-president of Iraq, by the Iraqi Judicial Council. Hashimi was accused of being a terrorist who had operated a hit squad against Shia political leaders. The warrant was based on very questionable testimony that had been obtained from his previously arrested bodyguards. Hashimi denounced the charges as fabrications and refused to turn himself in. He was subsequently granted asylum by the Turkish government and currently resides in Ankara. Other prominent Sunni leaders were also targeted. The unwillingness of the Iraqi government to either incorporate the Sunni militias into the military and police forces, or find another long term solution to give them meaningful employment and, more broadly, to continue to marginalize Iraqi Sunnis, would prove to be fertile ground for the Islamic State and set the stage for the return of an even more virulent and far reaching jihadist insurgency.

Postscript: The Rise and Fall of the Awakening Councils

When US combat forces withdrew from Iraq in August 2010, the country in general, and Anbar province in particular, had been largely pacified. The Shia insurgency in Baghdad and the south had ended and the bulk of the Badr militia had been absorbed into the Iraqi Army. Although some might argue that it was more of a case of the Iraqi Army being absorbed by the Badr militia and its leadership. The government was in control of the principal cities in Anbar and the other predominant Sunni provinces. There were still scores of jihadist organizations operating in Iraq, although Islamic State of Iraq was far and away the principal group and had managed to subsume much of the financial support and manpower of the other groups, but the tempo of their activity had been significantly reduced. Atrocities and human rights abuses still continued, promulgated by both the Iraqi government and its jihadist opponents, but these were directed at Iraqi citizens and generated little interest among Western governments or the international media. In Baghdad, in particular, a continuing policy of "ethnic cleansing" being carried out by Shia militants under cover of the Iraqi Interior Ministry, has seen the Sunni population drop from about 45 percent of the city's inhabitants in 2003 to less than 25 percent a decade later.[35]

In the inevitable post mortems that follow military interventions, there has been a great deal of speculation that had the US acted sooner to organize the Awakening Councils, or a similar type of organization, much of the turmoil and violence, and the accompanying American and Iraqi death toll, of the jihadist insurgency could have been avoided. There have been any number of Sunni leaders who have argued that they had approached Washington with solutions, in some cases even before the actual invasion took place. There is no question that the United States was better at waging war against Saddam Hussein than it was at managing the resulting peace. Countless mistakes were made, from the marginalization of Ba'athist party members and virtually all of the members of the previous government to the inability to ensure basic services once the occupation started, which, with the benefit of hindsight, are glaringly obvious. The argument that there were quicker, simpler solutions that the US failed to take advantage off, however, is simply not supported by the facts.

First, while there had been discussions with various Sunni leaders about potentially replacing Hussein, it is highly unlikely that such a coup would have succeeded. Despots stay in power because they are very good at ensuring that potential, would be, despots are eliminated before they can pose a threat. That has certainly been the pattern elsewhere in the Arab world and is underscored by the chaos that has accompanied the "Arab Spring" induced ousting of despots in Egypt, Libya, and, in part, Syria. Realistically, any replacement to Hussein would have had to come out of the army. The idea that Iraqi armed forces could have revolted in mass and replaced Hussein is naïve. The Republican Guard was deeply loyal to Hussein and was directly under his control. Much of the rest of the Iraqi Army was made up of poorly trained Shia draftees. They had little interest in fighting to replace one Sunni strongman with another.

Moreover, the "solutions" initially offered by the Anbar sheiks were "Sunni solutions" and would have resulted in the replacement of Saddam Hussein by another Sunni leader more acceptable to the West. It would not have really dealt with the disenfranchisement of the Shias and Kurds or the other minority groups. At best, it would have offered up a "kinder and gentler" version of Hussein; a sort of "Saddam light." Moreover, in the absence of a widespread military revolt, the Sunni civil war that would have resulted is unlikely to have succeeded in ousting of Hussein without the intervention of American troops. There was any number of Iraqi leaders, both Shia and Sunni who promised that, given political support and sufficient cash to work with, they could "solve" the post intervention chaos of Iraq. Some of them were given considerable prominence in the early months of the occupation by the White House. In the end none of them were able to deliver the "simple solution" that they had promised. In fact there was no "simple solution."

Only the intervention of American military forces would have succeeded in ousting Saddam Hussein. Whether in fact it was in the United States' long-term interest do so, is an altogether different question. In doing so the US had to decide whether to align itself with the Shia majority or a Sunni minority. It opted to do the former and in doing so it could not help but make the Sunni minority deeply suspicious of its motives and apprehensive of their long-term role in a post Hussein, Shia dominated, Iraq. Had it done the latter, it would only have succeeded in trading a Sunni insurgency for a much larger, and ultimately more problematic, Shia insurgency. While there was significant opposition to Hussein between both Shia and Sunni groups, the two sides had little in common and no shared consensus on what a post Hussein Iraq would look like or how it would be governed. The notion that centuries of ill treatment of Shias by the Sunni minority could be set aside in a new "reconciliation government" was beyond just naïve. It evidenced a complete disregard of Iraqi history, Shia-Sunni relations, and the political dynamics of the contemporary Middle East.

Could the United States have moved sooner to support the organization of the Awakening Councils? The answer is yes, but it is important to note that we are speaking of months here, not years. To begin with, the organization of the Awakening Councils had to come from the Sunni community itself. It was not a solution that could be imposed by the US military. The one factor in the control of the United States was whether or not to arm the Sunni militias. Without arms, it was impossible for the Sunni community to offer much resistance to jihadist groups. Arming them made it more likely that the Sunni community would take the initiative and helped to accelerate a process that was already in formation. It should be kept in mind, however, that initially the Sunni community, especially in Anbar, had tolerated, if not actually supported, both the Ba'athist and then jihadist insurgency as a means of ensuring their relevancy in the post-Hussein Iraqi government. As noted earlier, the more Baghdad marginalized the Sunni community, the more Sunni leaders were willing to play their "control" of the "insurgency card" to ensure themselves a seat at the bargaining table. Whether the earlier organization and arming of Sunni militias would have preempted that support is unclear. Nor is it clear whether an earlier timetable for organizing the militias would have been politically feasible.

The "jihadist card" strategy ultimately failed because the objectives of the jihadists and those of the Sunni tribal leadership were fundamentally at odds. The tribal leaders wanted to ensure that the Sunni community received its "fair share" of political power in a post-Hussein Iraq while the jihadists wanted to ensure that any post-Hussein, Shia dominated, government would be still born. In the end, the Sunni leadership could not really "control" the jihadist insurgency much less turn it "on and off" as circumstances dictated, while the jihadists wore out their welcome by turning on the very Sunni community whose support, or at the very least acquiescence, they needed to operate. Their insistence on imposing a social order that had little support among the Sunni community and the increasing violence they brought to bear on both the community and its leadership at the slightest sign of opposition, coupled with the increasingly "foreign character" of the jihadists, eventually led to widespread public support for an anti-jihadist agenda. Even then, without the arming of the Sunni militias that initiative would have gone nowhere and functioned to simply make known to jihadists those Sunni leaders who were most opposed to them. Prior to the arming of the Sunni militias such opposition had been summarily dealt with. Even after the organization of the militias and the stepped up American military presence in Anbar, such opposition inevitably precipitated a jihadist attack.

Even then, the United States agreed to arm the Sunni militias, in the face of the Maliki government's opposition, because it was simply out of options. By 2006, Anbar province and its principal cities were in the control of jihadist groups, principally the Islamic State of Iraq. Any attempt by American and Iraqi forces to root them out would have produced significant civilian casualties and would in all likelihood have actually made the situation worse. The willingness of the Sunni community and its leadership to challenge the jihadists coincided perfectly with an American willingness to try a previously unacceptable solution, organizing and arming Sunni militias. The results of that strategy speak for themselves. What a pity that those successes would ultimately be squandered by the shortsighted policies of the Iraqi government.

Chapter 3

The "Arab Spring" and the Rise of Islamic State

The Jasmine Revolution and the Arab Spring

On December 17, 2010, a young Tunisian street vendor immolated himself in protest of the confiscation of his goods and the harassment by a local municipal official that he claimed had been inflicted on him. His suicide triggered a widespread campaign of civil disobedience in Tunisia, dubbed the Tunisian, or Jasmine Revolution, that within a matter of weeks would seek the ousting of longtime Tunisian President Zine El Abidine Ben Ali.

The events in Tunisia would be mirrored elsewhere in the Arab world and would result in the replacement of long standing governments in Tunisia, Egypt, and Yemen, a civil war in Syria and Libya, and widespread protests in Bahrain, Algeria, Iraq, Jordan, Kuwait, Morocco, Sudan, and among the Arab inhabitants of both Israel and the Palestinian territories. Additional, smaller protests broke out in Mauritania, Oman, Saudi Arabia, Djibouti, and Morocco's Western Sahara. The protests were motivated by a number of factors, from suppression of Sunni communities in Syria and in Iraq to the suppression of Shia majorities in Bahrain and Shia minorities elsewhere in the Gulf States. Some conflicts pitted Islamic or jihadist inspired groups against what they perceived as corrupt, unresponsive regimes, like Libya and Egypt, while others were triggered by a range of purely local causes.

Called the "Arab Spring" by media commentators, the movements were characterized by a sustained campaign of civil resistance involving demonstrations, marches, strikes, and rallies. All of the campaigns relied heavily on social media to mobilize support and communicate both with the media and among the demonstrators. The protests were often met with a heavy-handed response by government authorities. In Egypt, a government crackdown against the demonstrators would lead to the fall of Hosni Mubarak and to the election of a Muslim Brotherhood inspired government. Ultimately, that government would trigger a new round of civil protests that would result in its replacement in a military coup. In Syria, Yemen, and Libya, the protests triggered a civil war that still raged as 2015 began. Elsewhere civil disturbances have subsided through a combination of government repression, promises of reform, and governmental largess.

In Iraq, the Arab Spring triggered a range of protests that cut across the political and religious divide. In what came to be called the "Day of Rage," predominantly Shia protestors, on February 12, 2011, gathered in several major Iraqi cities, most notably Baghdad and Karbala, to protest government corruption, the inadequate provision of utilities and other government services, and the issue of inadequate national security. In an effort to head off the protests, Iraqi Prime Minister Nouri al-Maliki announced that he would not seek a third term as prime minister in 2014 and called for a constitutional amendment to limit terms in office. After the protests took place, the Iraqi government announced new subsidies on electricity costs. Protests continued intermittently over the next several months. On April 9, 2011, the eighth anniversary of the fall of the Hussein government in Baghdad, thousands demonstrated in Baghdad's Tahir Square, as well as around the country. On May 26, new demonstrations organized by Muqtada al-Sadr drew several hundred thousand protestors to Tahir Square.

In Iraqi Kurdistan, protests also took the form of anti-government demonstrations against the Kurdistan Regional Government over corruption and social injustice. Most of the protests were centered in the city of Sulaymaniyah. The demonstrators also demanded the immediate resignations of the cabinet and the disbanding of the regional government. Kurdish authorities cracked down on protestors, often using police to sweep them out of public squares. They also sought to intimidate journalists reporting on the demonstrations. A second series of riots occurred on December 2, 2011, triggered by "Friday sermons" from Muslim clerics, believed to be associated with the Kurdistan Islamic Union, calling for jihad against retailers selling alcohol and massage parlors in the northern town of Zakho. In response to the sermons, angry mobs destroyed Assyrian (Chaldean Christians) and Yezidi owned businesses causing several million dollars in damages in the towns of Zakho, Dohuk, Semel, and surrounding villages.

A new round of protests erupted on December 21, 2012. These demonstrations began in Fallujah and spread throughout the Sunni areas of Iraq. They were triggered by a raid on the home of Iraqi Finance Minister Rafi Hiyad al-Issawi and the arrest of ten of his bodyguards, as well as ongoing resentment by Sunnis of what they saw as their continued marginalization in Iraq. Earlier, in December of 2011, in response to claims by one of Maliki's advisors that al-Issawi had links to al-Qaida in Iraq, al-Issawi had begun to boycott cabinet meetings in protest. A US led investigation conducted in 2010 had concluded that earlier, similar allegations had been groundless. Al-Issawi later claimed that nearly 150 members of his staff and bodyguards had been arrested as part of a deliberate government attempt to harass him.

These protests were driven by claims that the Iraqi anti-terrorism laws were being abused and that Sunnis were being unfairly singled out for arrest and harassment. In addition, many Sunnis claimed that the "de-Ba'athification" laws were being used to unfairly confiscate property of former Ba'athists in the military and government. The protests also came during a time that the Baghdad government was attempting to dismantle the Awakening Councils and when it had yet to fulfill promises of integrating the Sunni militias into the armed forces. Moreover, members of Sunni militias claimed that they were being singled out and attacked by Iraqi Army forces.

On April 23, an Iraqi Army raid against an encampment of Sunni protestors in the city of Hawija, west of Kirkuk, resulted in the deaths of dozens of individuals and triggered a new round of demonstrations against the government. A number of jihadist groups used the incident to launch retaliatory attacks against Shia targets. The outbreak of sectarian violence, the worst since the withdrawal of US troops, would result in more than 300 deaths in the month of April. Protests continued through May, taking on an increasingly anti-government and anti-Maliki tone. In total several thousand civilians died during the six-month long demonstrations. The death toll reversed three years of steadily declining fatalities in Iraq. In retrospect it marked the end of the relatively peaceful interlude that followed the defeat of jihadist forces in Anbar, and the other Sunni dominated areas, that had been engineered by the Sunni militias and US ground forces and the beginning of a new round of sectarian violence that would see Islamic State militants take control of much of the Sunni areas of Iraq and which, as of the end of 2015, shows no signs of abating.

It was in Syria, however, that the Arab Spring would precipitate its deadliest consequences. Syria is an anomaly in the Sunni dominated politics of the Arab world. While a majority of its population is Sunni, the Assad family, members of the Shia Alawite sect, has ruled it for almost half a century, first by Hafez al-Assad (president from 1971-2000), and then by his son Bashir (from 2000 until present). The Alawites comprise just 12 percent of Syria's population. Until the period of the French mandate over Syria, 1919-1943, Alawites were subject to persecution by Sunnis. Under the French, Alawites were heavily recruited for the French Colonial Army in Syria and have remained a dominant presence in the Syrian Armed Forces ever since. When Assad took power in 1970, he reorganized the government and concentrated most of the political power in the Syrian presidency. Sunnis became the formal heads of the political institutions, while the Alawites were given control of the key military, security, and intelligence organizations.

Those organizations have been the key to the Assad family's continued hold on power in Syria.

Sunni unrest, centered originally on the Muslim Brotherhood in Syria, has been a prominent feature of Syrian politics and pre-dates the Assad family's rule. The Brotherhood's history dates back to World War II, and it was an important political party during the 1950s and early 60s. It was banned in 1963; a precondition imposed by Nasser for union with Egypt in the United Arab Republic, and has remained illegal since. From 1976 through 1982, the Brotherhood was at the center of a series of revolts and an insurgency by Sunni Islamists against the Assad government. In what came to be called a "long campaign of terror," Muslim insurgents carried out guerilla attacks in major cities across Syria against government and military officials. Assad's government responded with a heavy-handed repression, including mass arrests, torture, and summary execution of suspected militants. In one instance, after an attempt on Assad's life on June 26, 1980, Syrian military units responded by executing more than 1,200 Islamists imprisoned in Tadmor Prison.

The unrest culminated in the siege and subsequent massacre of civilians in the city of Hama, which lasted from February 2-28, 1982. Hama had long been a stronghold of the Muslim Brotherhood. It had been the scene of anti-Ba'ath party riots in 1963 and had been at the center of the Sunni uprising from 1976-1982. On February 3, the Muslim Brotherhood in Hama rose up in a citywide revolt against the Syrian government. By morning, more than seventy leading Ba'athist government officials had been killed and Syrian Army units stationed in Hama came under attack. Proclaiming Hama a "liberated city," the Muslim Brotherhood issued a statement urging Syrians to rise up against the "infidel" government. Assad responded by sending 12,000 troops to besiege the city and ordered air strikes and artillery bombardment against suspected insurgents and sympathizers.

The siege lasted for three weeks. The number of casualties has never been accurately determined. It is believed that between ten thousand and forty thousand people died during the siege although some estimates have placed the death toll at over one hundred thousand. There were also unconfirmed reports that Syrian forces used hydrogen cyanide gas against the militants. Much of the old city of Hama was destroyed. Thousands of additional civilians suspected of being members of the Muslim Brotherhood, or sympathizers, were rounded up and subjected to torture and summary execution. An additional one hundred thousand inhabitants of Hama were expelled from the city. Approximately one thousand Syrian soldiers were killed in the fighting. The destruction of Hama ended the Sunni uprising. It also gave rise to the expression, coined by New York Times reporter Thomas Friedman, "Hama Rules."[36] A shorthand way of saying that the Assad government would stop at nothing to put down revolts.

Sporadic violence continued in the intervening decades and was met with typically brutal repression. Syria has been under continuous martial law from 1963 until lifted by Assad, on April 21, 2011. The Syrian security agency, the Mukhabarat, has broad powers to arrest and detain indefinitely anyone deemed to be a threat to state security. In January 2011, minor protests, inspired by the "Arab Spring" elsewhere in the Arab world, began in Damascus and several other cities. The demonstrators were protesting what they saw as widespread government corruption and human rights abuses. The protests grew rapidly and by April quickly turned into massive anti-Ba'athist government demonstrations. The Assad government responded with its trademark brutality, unleashing police and military violence against the demonstrators, mass arrests, and intimidation. The brutal crackdown resulted in hundreds of deaths and thousands of wounded. The government did offer some concessions to the protestors including a reversal on the ban of teachers wearing the niqab and an end to the state of martial law that had existed since 1963. Assad also made vague promises for political reform including a reduction in the length of mandatory military service, the release of political prisoners, a reduction in taxes, increases in the salaries of public sector employees, and more press freedom. Many of these reforms were never actually implemented, however.

Syria: The Beginning of Civil War

Over the course of the spring of 2011, a number of militant opposition groups began to emerge. For the first time, there were also significant defections from the Syrian Army. By October 2011, US intelligence sources had estimated that around 10,000 Syrian soldiers had defected. Gradually, the civil uprising was transformed into an armed rebellion. On July 29, 2011, a group of Syrian Army officers who had defected proclaimed the creation of al-Jaish as-Suri al-Hurr (Free Syrian Army, FSA), and declared that their goal was to "bring this regime down." A few months later the FSA merged with the Harakat ad-Dubbat al-Ahrar (Free Officers Movement). Initially, 90 percent of the FSA consisted of Sunni Muslims that had been serving in the Syrian military. The FSA began to receive military support from the Turkish government in October 2011 and was allowed to set up its headquarters in the Turkish province of Hatay alongside the Syrian border.

In the meantime, a group of Syrian exiles had organized, in Istanbul, the al-Majlis al-Watani as-Suri (Syrian National Council, SNC). Initially the council denied that it was a "government in exile" but as the violence in Syria intensified, it increasingly assumed that role and announced that its objective was "the end of Bashar al-Assad's rule and the establishment of a modern, civil democratic state."[37] The SNC was organized into a General Assembly, a General Secretariat, and an Executive Board. Membership in the council was to include around 120 members representing all of the Syrian opposition groups, including organizations formed by Kurds, Christians, Druze, and other minority groups. In addition to its role as a "government in exile," the SNC's primary function was to secure financing and weapons to arm the rebels. The SNC's membership also included many members from the exiled Syrian branch of the Muslim Brotherhood and was receiving financial aid from the Turkish and Qatari governments. More than half of the members of the council were described as "Islamists," although none of the radical jihadist groups that would eventually emerge during the Syrian civil war were members.

Beginning in December 2011, the FSA began to coordinate its actions with the SNC. In January 2012, the SNC agreed to recognize the FSA and to provide funds to "keep the Free Syrian Army afloat." Military defections continued to mount and, for the first time, senior and staff officers were among the defectors. By March, the number of defections had increased to 60,000, and by July 2012 the number exceeded 100,000 and included a half dozen generals. In the meantime, a second military group, calling itself the Higher Revolutionary Council, had emerged. The group was led by General Mustafa Ahmad al-Sheikh, the highest-ranking defector from the Syrian Army.

From April 2011 through the end of 2012, a broad insurgency emerged throughout Syria, and attempts by Syrian rebels to hold towns and other urban areas were met with fierce resistance by Syrian military forces. Lacking any heavy weapons, including tanks and artillery, and without the benefit of any air power, the rebels found it impossible to mount an effective defense against the overwhelming military force that the Syrian Army could bring to bear. In Daraa, which had emerged as the most vocal center of the Syrian protests, the Syrian Army laid a siege that lasted from April 25 through May 16. For the final assault, the Syrian Army mobilized approximately 30 tanks, artillery, 6,000 troops, and helicopter deployed paratroopers against a force armed only with light weapons. The final assault resulted in the deaths of 244 civilians and 81 Syrian soldiers. Approximately 1,000 additional men were rounded up as "rebel sympathizers and suspected terrorists" and detained by the military. Similar sieges occurred in Baniyas (May 7-14, 2011), Tafas (May 11, 2011), and Talkalakh (May 14-19, 2011), among others. The city of Hama once again came under siege (July 3-August 4, 2011) and was subsequently attacked, resulting in the deaths of several hundred civilians. In Homs, the siege, by some 10,000 Syrian Army soldiers and 300 tanks, lasted for three years (May 6, 2011-May 9, 2014), before Free Syrian Army forces finally withdrew. The city was largely destroyed in the fighting. The extent of civilian casualties has never been determined.[38]

Lacking the ability to defend any of the urban centers over the course of 2011, the FSA and other rebel groups conducted a widespread insurgency against Syrian military forces and the allied, Shabiha (Ghost) militia. The Shabiha militia was predominantly Alawite militias, a combination of criminal gangs and military irregulars that were loyal to the Assad family. FSA operations consisted primarily of ambushes and IEDs targeted against military and militia forces, as well as against convoys bringing supplies and reinforcements to Syrian troops. At this point the conflict was predominantly Syrian in character. Neither Iran nor Hezbollah had yet intervened in a significant way on behalf of the Assad government. Nor were jihadist organizations prominent in the fighting. Hizb ut-Tahir (Party of Liberation), an international pan-Islamic political organization committed to the creation of an Islamic state or caliphate rule in accordance with Sharia law, had been present in Syria and had participated in some of the political demonstrations. The organization was political however, rather than military, and although it advocated the overthrow, both by democratic and military means, of democracies and dictatorships alike, it lacked any practical means of doing so. Beginning in 2012 however, jihadist elements would begin to make their presence in the Syrian Civil War known, and in the process transform the conflict from a purely domestic one into an international conflict.

On January 23, 2012, a group calling itself Jabhat an-Nusra li-Ahli ash-Sham (The Support Front for the People of Al-Sham), or simply the al-Nusra Front, announced that it was entering the Syrian Civil War against the Assad government.[39] Al-Sham, or Bilad al Sham, is Arabic for the region common called the "Levant." Nusra can be translated as "support." So al-Nusra Front means literally "the Support Front." The group is led by Abu Mohammad al-Julani. The name is believed to be a *nom de guerre*. His real name has never been revealed. He is believed to be of Syrian origin, from his accent, and to have come, based on his *nom de guerre*, from somewhere in the Syrian Golan

Heights. He was a teacher of Classical Arabic in Syria before leaving to become a jihadist in Iraq sometime in 2004.

Jihadists had actually first started appearing, in small numbers, in Syria, during 2011. In many cases, they were individuals that simply joined up with the Free Syrian Army or another one of the rebel groups. Al-Nusra is believed to have been the first of the jihadist groups to declare itself in Syria and commence operations. This development was not surprising. ISI was just across the border from Syria, a border that had traditionally been quite porous. Between late 2011 and the end of 2014, more than 50 jihadist groups announced their participation in the Syrian Civil War. Some like al-Nusra or its affiliate the Khorasan Group were well funded and could call on an experienced cadre of men. Others existed only on paper with little operational capabilities beyond issuing communiqués. Others still, consisted of little more than websites to raise funds and were, in fact, largely scams.

Originally, al-Nusra members were drawn largely from Sunni Islamist mujahedeen who had been part of Abu Musab al Zarqawi's network. Beginning sometime in late 2011, under orders from Abu Bakr al-Baghdadi, Emir of the Islamic State of Iraq (ISI), they began to be infiltrated into Syria. It does not appear they took part in any military operations, other than the suicide car bombing outside the offices of the Shu'bat al-Mukhabarat al-'Askariyya (Military Intelligence Directorate) in Damascus on December 23, 2011, before the existence of the group was announced. This was the first time suicide bombers had appeared in the Syrian Civil War. Beginning on January 6, 2012, however, they underscored their presence with a suicide bomber attack against a caravan of busses carrying riot police to a planned demonstration in Damascus. On February 10, 2012, two suicide car bombers attacked the Mukhabarat headquarters in Aleppo. Following in the patterns of other jihadist conflicts, suicide bombings quickly became part of the landscape of the Syrian conflict. Between December 2011 and June 2013, there were a total of 70 suicide bombings in Syria, 57 of which were carried out by al-Nusra jihadists.[40]

It is not entirely clear why the al-Nusra Front was organized as a separate organization. It's likely that its designation as an independent organization, one led by a Syrian jihadist, was an attempt to establish its "Syrian credentials" and minimize its foreignness. By separating it from its Iraqi parent, the organization would also not be automatically branded a terrorist organization. In fact, after the United States listed al-Nusra as a terrorist organization in December 2012, Moaz al-Khatib, the leader of the National Coalition for Syrian Revolutionary and Opposition Forces, the successor organization to the SNC, as well as 29 anti-Assad groups, called on the United States to reconsider its decision. On December 14, thousands of Syrians protested the American decision carrying banners declaring, "There is no terrorism in Syria except that of Assad."[41]

The FSA had been leery of the al-Nusra jihadists. While welcoming their support and acknowledging their help during the Battle for Aleppo against Syrian and Hezbollah military forces, some elements in the FSA had accused foreign jihadists of "hijacking a revolution that began as an uprising to demand a democratic system." One FSA leader summed up the concern by noting "we are not fighting Bashar al-Assad to go from living in an autocratic to a religious prison."[42] Equally concerning to the FSA had been the wholesale defection of some of its military units to al-Nusra. While ideology might have played a role in the defections, the better-financed al-Nusra could offer something the FSA couldn't—a steady paycheck. Al-Nusra played a major role in the FSA's siege and eventual capture (August 2, 2012-August 6, 2013) of the Syrian Air Base at Menagh. Suicide bombers supplied by al-Nusra, played a key role in the seizure of the base.

Al-Baghdadi and ISI Move Into Syria

In April 9, 2013, Abu Bakr al-Baghdadi, the "Emir" of the Islamic State of Iraq (ISI) released a recorded message via the internet in which he declared that Jabhat al-Nusra and ISI would be merging and that the resulting organization would henceforth be known as ad-Dawlah al-Islamiyah fi al-Iraq wash-Sham (Islamic State of Iraq and al-Sham), or ISIS.[43] In the communiqué Baghdadi announced that al-Nusra was simply the Syrian extension of al-Qaeda in Iraq and that its leader, Abu Mohammad al-Julani, and his men had been dispatched to Syria by Baghdadi to meet with preexisting ISI cells there. He went on to state that it was ISI's leadership that had provided al-Nusra's tactics and strategy and had been funding their operations on a monthly basis. The next day, al-Julani rejected the merger. He also reaffirmed al-Nusra's allegiance to Ayman al-Zawahiri and al-Qaeda. He went on to add, "neither al-Nusra command, nor its consultative council, nor its leader were aware of this announcement,"[44] and that they had not been consulted.

The next month, Baghdadi traveled to Syria and began openly recruiting members of al-Nusra to join ISIS military units. At the time, al-Nusra was one of the largest, if not the largest, of the jihadist groups operating in Syria. Many of al-Nusra's foreign fighters joined ISIS, while many of the remaining jihadist fighters left and joined other Islamist groups. ISIS's strength in Syria grew rapidly and by the end of the year it claimed to have the largest cadre of fighters against Assad. On June 9, Al Jazeera announced that it had obtained a copy of a letter that Zawahiri had sent to both Baghdadi and Julani in which he informed them that he had decided that the two organizations should remain separate and that he was appointing an emissary to oversee the two groups.[45] The name of the emissary was not disclosed. A week later, Baghdadi released another audio message where he rejected Zawahiri's decision and announced that the merger would be going ahead.[46] Tensions between Zawahiri and Baghdadi remained high and on February 2, 2014, Zawahiri expelled Baghdadi and ISIS from al-Qaeda and disavowed any links between the two organizations.[47]

Almost immediately, clashes broke out between ISIS and al-Nusra fighters and between ISIS and other rebel groups in Syria, both jihadist and others. The rebel groups in Syria had always been highly fragmented. There had been sporadic clashes between the FSA and various jihadist groups in prior years, but the intensity and frequency of those clashes now increased dramatically. In the meantime, starting in January 2014, the FSA and jihadists affiliated with the Islamic Front launched an offensive against ISIS in Aleppo. On February 26, 2014, Julani accused ISIS of the killing of a senior commander of Ahrar ash-Sham al-Islami (Islamic Movement of the Free Men of the Levant), and gave Baghdadi five days to submit evidence of their innocence to a panel of three jihadists clerics or Nusra would "go to war" against ISIS.[48] Ahrar ash-Sham (AS) claimed to be the largest jihadist group in Syria, notwithstanding ISIS's claims, and had between 10,000 and 20,000 fighters. Only the FSA was larger and AS was the principal group operating under the umbrella of al-Jabhat al-Islamiyah (Islamic Front). The Islamic Front was a coalition of seven different jihadist groups that were working together under Saudi sponsorship and were receiving financing and arms from them. Baghdadi ignored the challenge. On April 16, 2014, ISIS assassinated Nusra's chief in Idib province, Abu Muhammad al-Ansari, and his entire family.

Over the balance of 2014, open warfare erupted between ISIS and many of the other jihadist groups. In addition ISIS was also fighting the Free Syrian Army as well as Assad's military forces. Unlike the insurgency that had characterized the first phase of the Syrian Civil War, ISIS's intent now was the control of physical territory. On June 29, 2014, following the rapid conquest of large portions of western Iraq, including the city of Mosul, Baghdadi proclaimed a worldwide caliphate. Taking the title Emir al-Mu'minin (Leader of the Faithful), the traditional title of Muslim caliphs, he declared himself Caliph Ibrahim and renamed ISIS the ad-Dawlah al-Islamiyah (Islamic State), or IS. As Caliph of the Islamic State, Baghdadi now claimed religious, political, and military authority over all Muslims worldwide. Subsequent to the announcement, jihadist groups in the Sinai, Libya, and Algeria recognized the Islamic State as a Caliphate and pledged their allegiance to Baghdadi.

Postscript: Islamic State, al-Qaeda and the Leadership of International Jihadism

The promise of the Arab Spring quickly gave way to an Arab Winter of violence and political chaos. In Syria, early political demonstrations turned increasingly violent in the face of heavy handed government repression and by 2011 had erupted into all out civil war. The anti-Assad opposition was progressively radicalized and fragmented by the entry of different groups of Islamic jihadists who sought not just the overthrow of the Syrian government but the establishment of an Islamic state, although there was no consensus among them on what that would entail, governed in accordance with Sharia law. In the meantime, a range of foreign states jockeyed for influence among the various actors in the civil war, each in turn looking to either ensure the survival of the Assad government or shape the government that would replace it.

As the Syrian Civil War raged, a second less obvious struggle was taking place for the *de facto* leadership of the international jihadist movement. In 2005, Islamic State's predecessor, had eagerly sought Osama bin Laden's and al-Qaeda's approval for its leading role in the Iraqi insurgency. Now, eight years later, deprived of bin Laden, its charismatic leader, with its leadership forced into hiding by relentless attack from the United States and its allies, with its international network in tatters, and its ability to conduct terrorist strikes sharply degraded, Zawahiri and al-Qaeda found that Baghdadi could challenge al-Qaeda's leadership with impunity. Indeed, on declaring the creation of Islamic State as a worldwide caliphate it quickly drew recognition and proclamations of allegiance from jihadist movements in Sinai, Libya, Yemen, Pakistan, Saudi Arabia and Algeria. By the beginning of 2015, jihadist groups in Chechnya and Dagestan had also proclaimed their allegiance to IS.[49] In doing so, it was not only repudiating al-Qaeda's leadership of the international jihadist movement, but also declaring that IS and Baghdadi had now supplanted it.

In announcing the creation of the IS, not only did Baghdadi declare that international jihadism had a new center and leadership, he also tied inexorably together two hitherto, largely unrelated, conflicts: the civil war in Syria and the *de facto* civil war in Iraq. That act marked the apex of the internationalization of the Syrian Civil War. It also created a situation where two very different conflicts with two different sets of allies and opponents found, notwithstanding there many other differences, common ground in opposing Islamic State and its militants. There was little consensus, however, on what the post Islamic State landscape should look like. The linkages between the two civil wars thus imposed an additional layer of complexity in formulating policy and created a set of allies who agree on opposing IS, but little else, and whose unofficial alliance will be incredibly difficult to manage.

By announcing the creation of a new state, one that contained portions of both Syria and Iraq and declaring it as the nucleus of a worldwide caliphate, and by specifically repudiating "Sykes-Picot" and by extension the national frontiers that had resulted from that treaty, Baghdadi was making it clear that Islamic State's ambitions went far beyond the civil wars in Iraq and Syria, or even the replacement of those governments, and that it entailed nothing less than an entirely new political order for the Middle East.

Chapter 4

Internationalization of the Syrian and Iraqi Civil Wars

The conflict in Syria may have begun as a civil war between the Alawite Assad government and Sunni rebel groups, but it rapidly assumed international proportions. At the heart of the issue was the fact that the conflict quickly became a proxy for a larger Shia-Sunni conflict that pitted Iran and its Shia allies against Saudi Arabia, Turkey, and their Sunni supporters. In addition, the large role played by jihadist organizations within the Syrian opposition made the conflict relevant to America's and its European allies' large concerns of international Salafist terrorism. The conflict also became an issue in the increasingly strained American-Russian relationship as Russia sought both to maintain its historical relationship with the Assad government, while at the same time seeing the conflict as an opportunity to underscore its relevancy and great power status in the region.

It also added new issues in Turkey's complicated relationship with the Kurds, both those inside Turkey and those in Syria and Iraq. Moreover, for Washington, the merging of the conflicts in Syria and Iraq added an additional layer of complexity as transnational jihadists were simultaneously fighting against a government in Baghdad that the United States wanted to see retain power and a government in Damascus that the US was uncertain, at least without any visibility on the alternatives, if it wanted to see continue. Finally, the collapse of Iraqi Armed Forces, and the resulting intervention by Iranian military and paramilitary forces, added a further complication to Washington's relationship with Tehran, and had a bearing on both the White House's attitude towards the Assad Regime, a key Iranian ally, as well as its policy on Iran's nuclear development program.

Fittingly, the expression, "the enemy of my enemy is my friend" is attributed to Arab origins (although it has been suggested it may date back to fourth century BC India). That dictum, more often than not, seems to be the overriding factor in the ever-shifting coalition of alliances that has emerged from the conflicts in Syria and Iraq.

The "Iranian Shia Arc of Influence" and the Shia-Sunni Split

Islam has two major denominations, Sunni and Shia, and a number of other, smaller sects. Approximately 85 percent of the world's Muslims adhere to the Sunni branch and the other 15 percent to the Shia branch. Sunni's are the majority in most Muslim countries. Shias are in the majority in Iran, Iraq, Bahrain, Azerbaijan and, most likely now, in Lebanon. Indonesia has the largest population of Sunnis and Iran has the largest population of Shias. Pakistan has the second largest population of both Shias and Sunnis in the Muslim world. Shias are also a significant percentage of the Muslim population in Yemen and Kuwait.

The historic origins of the Shia-Sunni split began with an issue over the succession on the death of the Islamic prophet Muhammad in AD 632. Sunnis believe that the selection of Muhammad's rightful successor should be based on the consensus of the Muslim community, "Ummah," in accordance with the process set out in the Koran. Shias believe that Muhammad endorsed his cousin and son-in-law, Ali ibn Abi Talib, as his successor. Ali was married to Muhammad's daughter Fatimah so this line of succession would have preserved the leadership of the Muslim community in the descendants, through Ali and Fatimah, of the prophet.

Ali was eventually chosen as "caliph," leader or successor, of the Muslim community and led the Ummah from AD 656 to AD 661. He was the fourth of the caliphs that ruled the Muslim community following the death of Muhammad. These first four: Abu Bakr 632-634, Umar ibn al-Khattab 634-644, Uthman ibn Affan 644-656, and Ali ibn Abi Talib 656-661 are referred to as the Rashidun or "rightly guided caliphs," both for their piety and for the fact they were the only caliphs who actually knew Muhammad while he was alive. The dispute became a permanent schism when Umayyad Caliph Yazid I killed Hussein ibn Ali and his entire family, following the Battle of Karbala in AD 680. Over time, the split led to differences in religious practices, customs and jurisprudence, which further divided the two communities.

The rise of the Safavid dynasty in Persia, today's Iran, in 1501, led to the establishment of the Shia branch of Islam as the official religion of the Safavid-Persian Empire. The Safavid dynasty was not the first Shia ruler of Persia, nor was it the first Shia ruler in the Muslim world. The Fatimid dynasty, which claimed to be direct descendants of Muhammad's daughter Fatima, ruled an Islamic Empire that stretched along the eastern and southern coast of the Mediterranean, including Egypt, Sudan, and Sicily, from 909-1171. The association of Shia Islam with Persia, however, added a geopolitical element to what had up to then been a purely religious difference. The rise of the Ottoman Empire in the sixteenth and seventeenth centuries often pitted the Ottoman-Sunni Empire against its Persian-Shia rival. Indeed, in the sixteenth century, at the height of the Christian-Ottoman rivalry for control of the Mediterranean, Phillip II, the Spanish Emperor of the Holy Roman Empire even proposed to the Safavids a Catholic-Shiite alliance against the Sunni Ottomans.

The Ottoman conquest of much of the Arab Middle East saw Sunni Arabs rise to positions of influence within the Ottoman Empire. Even within regions that were predominantly Shia, like Iraq, Sunnis were inevitably appointed to positions of power within the local government. Following the collapse of the Ottoman Empire after the First World War, the Anglo-French division, in accordance with the Sykes-Picot Treaty of 1917, preserved the predominance of Sunnis within the political hierarchy of the Middle East. Even with independence, predominantly Shia countries like Iraq still found themselves being ruled by a minority, Sunni elite. Iran, which had emerged from the Qajar dynasty of the historic Persian Empire, had under the Pahlavi dynasty styled itself a modern secular state. While the country remained predominantly Shia, the Iranian government did not see the promotion or defense of Shia minorities elsewhere as a concern.

The Iranian revolution, which began in 1978, and the establishment of an Islamic Republic in 1979, restored the close association between Shiism and a political state. From the very beginning of its existence, the Islamic Republic concerned itself with the plight of Shia communities and saw its influence in those communities as a source of political and diplomatic leverage. Iran has been a consistent supporter of Hezbollah, a Shiite organization, and was involved with its founding in 1982. It also has been a strong supporter of both Hamas and Islamic Jihad even though both of those organizations are predominantly Sunni in composition. Moreover, the Iranian Quds Force has been heavily involved with the training of Shiite militias and guerilla groups around the world.

Iran was also a steadfast supporter of the Assad government in Syria. The two countries shared a common foe in Saddam Hussein's Iraq and both were committed in thwarting Hussein's goal of making Iraq a regional power. They also shared a common enemy in the United States and Israel, and shared a common interest in using Hezbollah and Hamas as a vehicle for thwarting US plans for a Mid-East peace and to promote their own interests. From a practical standpoint, the uniformity of interests between the Assad government and the Islamic Republic were independent of the Shia roots of the Syrian Alawite government, but nonetheless, it fit nicely with Iran's view of itself as a defender of Shiite interests around the world.

Iranian Involvement in Syria and Iraq

Iranian involvement in the Syrian civil war began almost immediately with the "Arab Spring" inspired protests in Damascus. As early as March 2011, as the demonstrations in Syria were starting to gain momentum, there were reports of Iranian personnel assisting Syrian security officials.50 In addition, Iran provided Damascus with riot control equipment and trained Syrian security personnel in procedures for gathering intelligence on the protest movement.[51] Tehran also supplied technology that it had developed to monitor email, cell phones, and social media following the Iranian election protests in 2009-10. Following those protests, the Iranian government, some contend with the assistance of China, developed a cyber-army to track down and monitor online dissidents.[52]

In May 2012, according to a report in *The Guardian*, the Deputy Head of the Quds Force confirmed that they had provided combat troops to support Syrian military operations against the Syrian rebels.[53] Iran was also supplying Syria with diesel fuel and arms. Over the course of 2012, there was a sharp increase in the amount of arms shipments from Iran to Syria. Washington complained to Baghdad about its willingness to allow Iranian arms shipments to transit Iraqi airspace.[54] A UN report found that Iran was, in violation of sanctions imposed on Syria, and was in fact the principal supplier of arms to the Assad government.[55] In the summer of 2012, reports emerged that Tehran had dispatched additional units of the Quds Force to organize and train a pro-Assad militia in Syria.[56] In October, FSA militants displayed Iranian built drones, complete with training manuals, indicating they belonged to the Iranian Revolutionary Guards, which they claimed were being used to guide Syrian military planes in attacks on rebel positions.[57]

In June 2013, Robert Fisk, writing in *The Independent*, disclosed that Iran was sending 4,000 Revolutionary Guards troops to Syria and that this was only "the first contingent." There was also a report that Tehran had offered more troops to open up a new Syrian front against Israel in the Golan Heights but that the Assad government had declined the offer.[58] The extent of the Quds force deployed in Syria is not clear. As of the end of 2014, this force was believed to be at least 10,000 and possibly much higher.[59] The Quds force was under the command of Iranian General Qassem Soleimani and included over 70 Quds field commanders. Not all of these troops, however, were directly involved in the civil war. Iran had between 2,000 and 3,000 Quds Force soldiers stationed in the Syrian city of Zabadani. The city was Iran's logistical hub for supplying Hezbollah forces in Lebanon with arms and cash, and also hosted important training facilities for Hezbollah militants.[60]

Iranian support for the Assad government continued during 2014. Tehran has continued to send thousands of military specialists and Quds Force personnel, as well as volunteers from the Iranian Basji and Iraqi Shia Militias.[61] The Iranian government has also provided the Assad government with considerable financial assistance. According to a report by *The Economist*, that financial assistance had, by February 2012, reached nine billion dollars.[62] It is believed that the level of Iranian financial assistance had reached between 15 billion and 20 billion dollars by the end of 2014.[63]

The overthrow of Saddam Hussein's Ba'athist government resulted in the emergence of a Shia dominated government in Baghdad. Many of the Shia leaders that emerged in the wake of the American led invasion had strong ties to Iran and its political and religious leadership. Early on, Iran provided funding and military training for Shiite militias in Iraq. They also provided funding for a number of Shiite political parties. They played a critical role in supporting both Shiite and, to a lesser extent, Sunni elements of the anti-American insurgency that existed from 2003 through 2009. Iraq was to prove the linchpin in an area of Iranian influence among predominantly Shiite governments and organizations that stretched across Iraq, Syria, Lebanon, and the Gaza Strip. This zone has been variously described as an Iranian or Shiite "Arc of Influence" and its existence was seen as underscoring a "Shia revival" that had begun with the Iranian Revolution. The emergence of this "Shia Arc" also coincided with a period of renewed Iranian assertiveness in the Middle East in general and in the Persian Gulf in particular. The overthrow of Saddam Hussein, and his replacement with an Iraqi Shiite government friendly to Tehran, had eliminated what had been an existential threat to the Islamic Republic and had tipped the local balance of power significantly in Tehran's favor. The other Arab countries in the Gulf lacked the population or the armed forces, without American support, to be an effective deterrent to Iranian ambitions in the region.

In June of 2014, in response to the advances of Islamic State in Iraq and the virtual collapse of Iraqi military forces, Iran began to provide direct military aid to the Iraqi government. Iran immediately deployed 500 Quds Force soldiers to stiffen Iraqi positions in Samarra, Baghdad, and Karbala, as well as the former US base, Camp Speicher, in Tikrit.[64] The Iranian Revolutionary Guard also deployed seven Sukhoi, Soviet era, Su-25 Frogfoot jets. They also began to supply arms and munitions to Peshmerga forces in Kurdistan.[65] Significantly, Iranian General Soleimani was transferred to Baghdad where he assumed the position of "chief tactician" in the struggle with IS. Soleimani has often been seen on the battle line and is reported to be commanding both Iranian and Iraqi forces in the field.[66] In addition, Quds Force personnel set up a headquarters at the al-Rasheed Air Base, on the outskirts of Baghdad, to operate Iranian Abadil drones over Iraq as well as to intercept communications between IS and its field commanders.[67] At the same time, Hezbollah took on the responsibility of training Iraqi Shia Militias and deployed between 250 and 1,000 personnel to organize and supervise their training.[68]

Iranian military deployment increased further during the summer of 2014, despite continued Iranian denials that there were any Iranian troops stationed in Iraq. On August 21, Iran's 81st Armored Division took part in a joint Iranian-Kurdish attack to liberate Jalawla from IS militants.[69] In December 2014, Iran allowed foreign media to confirm the presence of Iranian F-4 Phantom jets in Iraq striking IS positions in Diyala province.[70] US sources later confirmed that the planes were Iranian but that US military forces were not coordinating air strikes with the Iranian military.[71] Although the presence of the F-4 Phantoms was not disclosed till December, these were not the first Iranian planes to be operating in Iraq and it is likely that the F-4s had been operating there for some time. In total, Iran had more than 1,000 military advisors in Iraq at the beginning of 2015 and had provided more than one billion dollars in military aid during 2014.[72] The actual number of Iranian military personnel in Iraq is actually much higher. Many of the Iranian military forces in Iraq are classified as volunteers. Moreover, some of the Iranian military units are stationed in Iran and move back and forth across the border as needed.

Foreign Involvement in the Syrian Civil War

The Syrian Civil War was quickly seen by the Sunni Arab states, especially Saudi Arabia and its Gulf allies, and to a lesser extent Turkey, as an opportunity to "roll back" the arc of Iranian influence in the Middle East. That opportunity brought political and financial support for the Free Syrian Army from Saudi Arabia and Qatar as well as the other Gulf states. It also brought financial assistance from wealthy donors and Islamic charities, some of which went to more radical groups that had begun operating in Syria. The emergence of more radical jihadist groups in the Syrian civil war was a source of concern for the United States, which feared, quite correctly, that jihadist violence in Syria could spill over into Iraq and potentially destabilize the country.

Russia has had a long-standing relationship with the Assad government that goes back decades. The Russian navy has a base in the Syrian city of Tartus. The naval base goes back to the Soviet era and is the only foreign military base outside the former Soviet Union. Russia has remained Syria's chief source of weapons, either directly or via Iran, and it has continued to train Syrian soldiers in their use. In 2012, there were news reports that "Russian military advisors" were in Syria and were manning some of the anti-aircraft defensive systems that had been provided by Russia.[73] As the civil war intensified, Moscow has stepped up its military support for Damascus and has provided a broad array of new weaponry including armored vehicles, laser guided bombs, surveillance equipment, and electronic warfare systems.[74] Russia has attempted to use its political influence in Syria as a bargaining chip in its broader agenda with the United States. It has proposed, on several occasions, diplomatic initiatives to "resolve" the violence in Syria, but, to date, it has not been successful in leveraging its influence in Syria in any meaningful way.[75] The fact is that while the Assad regime is dependent on Russia for advanced weaponry and diplomatic support, Russia does not have the ability to deliver Assad as part of any broader "peace agreement." The best that it can expect to do is to ensure that if the Syrian government is replaced, it can continue to retain influence in Syria post-Assad and maintain access to the naval facilities in Tartus.

Hezbollah has been closely allied with the Assad government from its very beginning and is dependent on Syria for much of its weaponry, including those weapons that originate in Iran. Hassan Nasrallah, Hezbollah's leader, has denied reports that Hezbollah has 3,000 fighters in Syria, although he has admitted that "volunteers" from Hezbollah have gone there independently to fulfill their "jihadist duties."[76]

Two unexpected players in the Syrian Civil War have been Venezuela and North Korea. Venezuela, while Hugo Chavez was in power, supplied Syria with millions of gallons of diesel fuel, on at least four separate occasions, between 2010 and 2012. It is not clear whether that assistance has continued since Chavez's death.[77] North Korea has historically supplied arms to Syria. Although such shipments are in violation of international sanctions, they have continued via a complex set of intermediaries that disguise the source and contents of the arms shipments. There have been reports in South Korean media that Arabic speaking advisors from the Korean People's Army have been advising the Syrian military.[78] The Syrian Observatory for Human Rights has also claimed that 15 North Korean pilots are operating combat helicopters in Syria.[79]

The Iraqi government has provided financial and material assistance to Syria, although the amount of that assistance is unclear. A number of leading Iraqi leaders, including former Prime Minister Maliki, have long standing ties with Syria. Maliki spent 15 years in exile in Syria. Iraq has allowed transit of Iranian planes carrying arms and supplies to the Syrian government. There were a number of joint Syrian-Iraqi military operations designed to secure the border areas and western Anbar province from jihadists. The extent of the current cooperation between the two countries is unclear at the moment, although it is fair to say that both governments see themselves combating a common foe in IS. There have been reports of additional assistance to the Syrian government being offered by a number of other countries and groups, including Algeria, the Houthi, Partisans of God militia, in Yemen, and Shiite groups in Lebanon. The extent of this assistance is unclear, however, and in any case it does not appear to be material. IS has claimed that it is holding prisoners from the Lebanese Army. What role the Lebanese Army has played in the Syrian Civil War is not apparent nor is the extent of its involvement.

The al-Jaish al-Iraqi al-Hurr (Free Iraqi Army, FIA) is a Sunni militant group organized among Sunnis in Iraq, which has been fighting in Syria under the umbrella of the Free Syrian Army. The group claims that it has approximately 2,500 members. The FIA claims it is opposed to both the Assad regime and the Shia dominated government in Baghdad. It also claims to be opposed to AQI, although the Iraqi government has accused it of being an AQI front. Kata'ib Hezbollah (Hezbollah Battalions) and the Jaish al-Mukthar (Mukthar Army) have specifically targeted the group, both organizations are Shia militia groups in Iraq organized and supported by the Quds Force. Both militias claim to be loyal to the Supreme Leader of Iran, Ayatollah Ali Khamenei. Both groups are listed as "terrorist organizations" by the US State Department. Ironically, in an illustration of the often unlikely alliances that are forming around opponents of Islamic State, both groups received close air support from US Air Forces during the battle for the Iraqi town of Amerli with IS militants.[80] Pentagon sources claim that there was no direct coordination with the Hezbollah brigades and that they simply took advantage of air strikes that had been launched to help Peshmerga forces attempting to break the siege of Amerli.[81]

Saudi Arabia and Qatar have been the two principal Arab supporters of the Syrian rebels. In addition, a number of the smaller Gulf States have also provided financial aid. The Arab League, at their Summit in Doha, on March 6, 2013, recognized the National Coalition for Syrian Revolutionary and Opposition Forces, as the only representative body of the Syrian people. Two weeks earlier, they had given a "green light" to supply aid to the Syrian rebels, although such aid had started in 2012.[82] According to a report in the *Financial Times*, Qatar had supplied over three billion dollars in aid through early 2013.[83] It is believed an additional two billion dollars in cash and arms was supplied between 2013 and the end of 2014.[84] There have been over 100 cargo flights of weapons from Qatar via Turkey to the Syrian rebels. In addition, it's believed that Qatar operates a training facility, in conjunction with the Central Intelligence Agency, for the training of Syrian rebels.[85] Approximately 2,000 rebels have gone through the three-week course. Starting in December 2012, Saudi Arabia began financing the purchase of heavy weapons for the Syrian rebels. These weapons included the Yugoslav designed M79 OSA recoilless anti-tank gun currently manufactured in Croatia. The Saudis also supplied light infantry weapons and ammunition.[86] These weapons were transferred to the rebels through Jordan underscoring the importance of controlling the few border posts in the relatively road less region of western Iraq. Much of the financing went to pay the monthly salaries for Syrian rebels. These typically averaged around 50 to 100 dollars per week, although they were higher for experienced officers. In addition, defectors from the Syrian Army were being offered bonuses, depending on their rank, of as much as 50,000 dollars.

The Saudi government, in August 2013, appointed Prince Bandar bin Sultan, a former ambassador to the United States (1983-2005) and Director General of the Saudi Intelligence Agency, to direct Saudi Arabia's effort to help the Syrian rebels. He stepped down as the Intelligence Chief and Special Envoy to the Syrian opposition on April 15, 2014. Ostensibly, the resignation was for health reasons, although there were reports that the White House had complained to the Saudis that bin-Sultan had been unnecessarily confrontational in trying to resolve policy differences over helping the Syrian rebels.[87] There were also concerns that some of the aid had gone to jihadist groups that the US opposed. The Saudis also set up a training facility in Jordan, headed by bin Sultan's half-brother, Salman bin Sultan, for the Syrian rebels. In January 2015, the United States announced that it was sending 400 troops to train Syrian fighters at camps in Saudi Arabia, Qatar and Turkey.[88] Collectively, Saudi Arabia, Qatar, and their Gulf allies had, as of the end of

2014, supplied in excess of 10 billion dollars in aid to the Syrian rebels.

One of the primary objectives of the Saudis and their allies was to organize the various groups into larger coalitions. Partly this objective was driven by the need to "bulk up" some of the other smaller Islamic groups so that they could better resist the larger forces of the Syrian government and the Islamic State. Larger coalitions would also reduce the amount of duplication between the various groups and reduce competition among them, especially the efforts of the various groups to recruit each other's members. The coalitions themselves were rather fluid, with member organizations joining and leaving, and in some cases being expelled, by the other members for various improprieties—theft being the most often sited reason for expulsion. In some cases specific groups could belong to more than one coalition at a time. The largest group organized was the Jaish al-Islam (Army of Islam, JAI).

JAI was a coalition of 43 different Syrian rebel groups. Estimates of its strength ranged from as little as 5,000 men to as many as 50,000. The coalitions excluded those groups directly linked to al-Qaeda, like Jabhat al-Nusra, but did include both Salafist and non-jihadist rebel groups. The Army of Islam was led by Zahran Alloush, a Salafist jihadist. He was also the head of Liwa al-Islam (Banner or Flag of Islam).[89]

Among the other coalitions formed were the Salafist group Harakat Ahrar ash-Sham al-Islami (Islamic Movement of the Free Men of the Levant, IMFML), who's substantial funding came almost exclusively from wealthy donors in Kuwait.[90] IMFML were briefly part of the Islamic Front, but then left. It is one of the groups that have been targeted by US air strikes. Another group, supported primarily by Qatar, was the Suquor al-Sham (Falcons of the Levant Brigade, FLB). The Jabhat Thowar Suriyya (Syrian Revolutionary Front, SRF) was an alliance formed in December 2013 composed of Free Syrian Army units as well as non-jihadist groups fighting in the Syrian Civil War. Its organization was in response to the organization of al-Jabhat al-Islamiyah (Islamic Front, IF), a coalition of seven groups also backed and armed by Saudi Arabia. As 2015 began the Syrian Civil War continued to show a never-ending kaleidoscope of rebel groups and ever-shifting alliances. Aid donors continued to push for broader coalitions, while at the same time competing amongst each other to have the largest and most effective group among the rebels, in order to ensure their influence in a post-Assad Syria.[91]

Turkey's role in the Syrian Civil War has been particularly complex. It was an early supporter of the Free Syrian Army. It allowed the FSA and its head, Colonel Riad al-Assad, to set up offices in Istanbul, and it supplied arms and financing equipment. Indeed, Turkey's Milli İstihbarat Teşkilatı (National Intelligence Organization, MIT), and its director, Hakan Fidan, played a major role in the organization and birth of the FSA in July 2011. Turkey has hosted, in Istanbul, both the National Coalition for Syrian Revolutionary and Opposition Forces, and its predecessor the Syrian National Coalition. Starting in May 2012, MIT also began the training some of the Syrian rebels.[92]

On the other hand, Ankara has been reluctant to be seen as acting in concert with the United States. Notwithstanding its early and continuing support for the FSA and other Syrian rebel groups, the Turkish government has refused the United States permission to stage strikes in Syria from Turkish airbases. It had also been concerned about the widening role of Kurdish groups in the fight against IS, and was resistant to allowing Peshmerga forces from Iraqi Kurdistan to cross Turkish territory to come to the aid of Syrian Kurds during the siege of Kobani. Eventually, however, Ankara did permit Iraqi Kurd reinforcements and supplies to come to the aid of their brethren in Kobani.

Turkey's relations with Iraqi Kurdistan and the Kurds in Syria is particularly complicated, especially given Ankara's own complex relationship with Turkey's Kurds and, until recently, with a long running Kurdish insurgency within Turkey. Ankara has supported the efforts of the Kurdistan Regional Government to export oil from fields under its control via Turkey. From the Turkish government's perspective, good relations with the predominantly Sunni Kurds in Iraq gives it influence within Iraq and potential leverage with the government in Baghdad. It also helps ensure that Iraqi Kurdistan does not become a safe haven for the Partiya Karkeren Kurdistan (Kurdistan Workers Party, PKK). Notwithstanding its relationship with the Kurdistan Regional Government, however, it's estimated that there are about 3,000 members of the PKK in Iraqi Kurdistan, between one-third and one-half of the PKK's total strength.

There have been numerous instances of Turkish military incursions into Iraqi Kurdistan in pursuit of PKK militants and even an occasional clash with Peshmerga forces along the border areas. The PKK has, at Ankara's insistence, historically been considered a terrorist organization. Its participation in the campaign against the Islamic State, however, may lead, much to Ankara's alarm, in having the United States remove the PKK from its list of "terrorist" organizations. Turkey's biggest concern is that the growing links between Iraqi and Syrian Kurds, the Kurdish Regional Government's desire to seek independence, and the continuing turmoil in Syria, could lead to the creation of an independent Kurdish state and to renewed demands by Turkish Kurds to either be part of an independent Kurdish state or have more autonomy for the Kurdish region within Turkey.

Support for the Syrian rebels also become an issue in Turkish-American relations. Ostensibly, both governments are in agreement to support the Syrian rebels. Ankara wants the White House to come out firmly in favor of the removal of Assad from power and wants US and allied air strikes to target Syrian Military Forces. Through 2014, US air strikes have been directed primarily against the Islamic State's forces and, to a lesser extent, at al-Qaeda affiliated jihadist groups. Initially, Washington was quite vocal in condemning Assad's attacks on Syrian civilians and even specified a "red line" that would prompt American intervention if Assad used chemical weapons in the conflict. It does appear that chemical weapons have been used in the Syrian Civil War, although by which side is debatable. In any case, it was only the collapse of Iraqi military forces fighting the Islamic State that finally prompted an American response. Lately, however, the White House has been ambivalent about its position regarding the future of the Assad government. Turkey is concerned that in order to secure Iranian assistance in pushing back Islamic State forces in Iraq, Washington will agree to take the overthrow of the Assad regime "off the table." For all practical purposes this has already occurred. Given how fluid the situation in Iraq and Syria is, however, American acquiescence to the continuation of the Assad regime could change very quickly.

One of the most unusual factors in Turkey's role in the Syrian Civil War concerns the status of the Tomb of Suleiman Shah. Suleiman is the grandfather of Osman I, the founder of the Ottoman Empire in 1299. His tomb is in Syria, near Aleppo, and is about 20 miles from the Turkish frontier with Syria. In accordance with Article 9 of the Treaty of Ankara signed in 1921 between France and the Turkish Republic, the tomb and the immediate area around it, is sovereign Turkish territory. The Turkish flag flies over the site and the Turkish military has historically maintained an honor guard of between 15 and 30 soldiers there. On March 20, 2014, ISIS threatened to attack the site unless Turkish troops were immediately removed. Ankara responded by increasing the number of troops stationed there. The next week, there were numerous reports in Turkish media that the Turkish government would use an attack on Suleiman's tomb as a pretext to intervene militarily in the Syrian Civil War.[93] On October 2, 2014, specifically citing the threat that Islamic State might capture the tomb of Suleiman Shah, the Turkish Parliament authorized the use of Turkish military force against IS.

As of January 2015 however, Turkish troops had not been deployed against IS militants in Syria.

The US Role in the Syrian and Iraqi Civil Wars

The involvement of the United States in the Syrian Civil War officially began in June 2014, when President Barack Obama authorized American air strikes against Islamic State militants as well as other radical jihadist groups operating in Syria and Iraq. At that time Obama also urged other countries to join the effort in a broad, multinational effort to help the Syrian rebels and "degrade" the military capabilities of IS. In reality a limited American involvement began much earlier. Almost from the very beginning of the outbreak of the Syrian Civil War there was an extensive debate within the Obama Administration over what assistance, if any, the US should provide to the Syrian rebels.

In March of 2012, President Obama requested the Pentagon to prepare a range of military options to help the Syrian rebels. According to the Chairman of the Joint Chiefs of Staff, General Martin Dempsey, the options considered ranged from humanitarian airlifts of food and medical supplies, to sharing intelligence on Syrian military plans and capabilities with the rebels, to the establishment of an actively patrolled "no-fly zone" over Syria. In early June 2012, pursuant to a presidential order authorizing support for the Syrian rebels, the CIA collaborated in setting up a "nerve center" in Adana, Turkey, to direct military aid to the Syrian rebels. The base was at Adana, Turkey about 60 miles from the Syrian border. Adana also hosts the Incirlik Air Force base where the US maintains a sizeable military presence and supply depot as well as broad intelligence gathering capabilities.[94]

At about the same time, the White House authorized 15 million dollars, later increased to 25 million dollars, in "non-lethal" aid via a State Department humanitarian relief program. This aid consisted of medical supplies, communications equipment and light trucks. It also directed the Pentagon to prepare a list of additional military options.[95] The military aid was being provided chiefly by Saudi Arabia, Qatar, and Turkey. It does not appear that at this point any military supplies were coming from the US. The CIA's role was to help coordinate the effort and, most likely, to try to ensure that aid was provided to rebel groups that the US deemed "acceptable."

Later that summer, during a press conference at the White House, President Obama declared that humanitarian aid to Syria had reached 82 million dollars and, while declining a "military response," noted that it would be, "a red line for us if we start seeing a whole bunch of chemical weapons moving around or being utilized." Adding, "That would change my calculus."[96] The White House, however, turned down a proposal presented by David Petraeus, the Director of the CIA, and supported by Defense Secretary Leon Panetta and the Joint Chiefs of Staff, to begin arming the Syrian rebels over concerns that the weaponry might fall into the hands of jihadists and that it might draw the US further into the Syrian Civil War.[97]

In an effort to marginalize jihadists, as well as provide broad political legitimacy to the Syrian rebels, the United States, Saudi Arabia, and other Arab supporters of the Syrian rebels urged the creation of the National Council of Syrian Revolutionary and Opposition Forces. In addition, a Revolutionary Military Council was organized under the National Council to coordinate the operations of the various rebel groups and to "unite units of Free Syrian Army, various militias and brigades in each city and large groups of defectors," and to funnel military aid to the rebels.[98] Concurrently, the CIA began a program in Jordan and Turkey to train Syrian rebels, with particular emphasis on antitank and antiaircraft weaponry. At the same time, the US government began supplying both arms and nonlethal aid directly to the Syrian rebels.[99]

US aid steadily increased during 2013, and is believed to have reached several hundred million dollars. This was in addition to several billion dollars of aid that was being supplied by Saudi Arabia, Qatar, and their Gulf allies. At the same time, the CIA began to supply "actionable intelligence" to rebel groups to use against Syrian government forces.[100] In response to the disarray of the Syrian rebels and the growing strength of the more radical jihadist groups, especially the al-Qaeda linked al-Nusra Front, the US began directly arming specific rebel groups. Reports that the Assad government had used Sarin gas in an attack against the rebels on August 21 almost precipitated an American cruise missile attack against military targets in Syria. The White House backed off the response when Great Britain and other NATO allies declined to participate in the attack. Instead the White House seized on a Russian proposal to secure and transfer, under U.N. supervision, any chemical weapons out of Syria.[101]

Support for the Syrian rebels mounted steadily over the first half of 2014. According to the US State Department, non-lethal aid, including assistance to neighboring countries for support of refugees from their Syrian fighting, had reached two billion dollars by June of 2014.[102] In the meantime, in March of 2013, the European Union agreed to lift the arms embargo against supplying weapons to the Syrian rebels and agreed that member states could provide arms and training.[103]

In response to the gains of the Islamic State in Iraq, in June 2014 the White House requested congressional funding of 500 million dollars to arm and train "appropriately vetted groups" within the Syrian opposition. It also requested an additional five billion dollars in antiterrorism funding to assist a number of Middle East countries in dealing with terrorist threats.[104] At the same time, on June 15, the White House declared than the United States would lead a multinational effort of targeted air strikes against Islamic State and other jihadist militants in Syria and Iraq. Originally, in what was likely an attempt to downplay the significance of the military campaign, no code name was assigned to the operation. On October 15, the campaign was retroactively called Operation Inherent Resolve. The name covers both the interventions in Iraq and in Syria against IS.

On June 15, the Iraqi government requested assistance in coping with the offensive from Islamic State militants. In response, on June 29, the White House immediately dispatched 300 soldiers to defend the Baghdad International Airport from attack by IS forces. The US also stepped up drone surveillance over Baghdad. The surveillance was in addition to an ongoing program over Iraq, which had been in operation since 2013, to track jihadist activity.[105] An additional 800 troops were dispatched to beef up the defense of the American Embassy in Baghdad and the US Consulate in Erbil amid reports that Islamic State militants had been training for an assault on the US embassy in Baghdad. Despite Pentagon concerns that many Iraqi military units were infiltrated by either Sunni or Shia extremists and that the embedding of US military personnel in such units would put them in danger, the White House, on August 5, directed US military forces in Iraq to "assess and advise" Iraqi forces in their conflict with IS militants.[106]

On August 5, the US began to directly supply Kurdish Peshmerga forces with arms. On August 7, in response to the IS siege that had trapped some 40,000 Yezidi and Christian refugees on Sinjar mountain, the US began aerial drops of food and water to the trapped refugees. That same day, President Obama announced that he was authorizing air strikes against IS militants surrounding Sinjar mountain and those threatening to advance on Erbil, the capital of the Kurdish Autonomous Region.

The next day, US Navy McDonnell Douglas F/A-18 Hornet fighters struck IS militants. A total of 162 air strikes were conducted in Iraq by the United States in conjunction with its allies in Operation Inherent Resolve between August 8 and September 16. In a letter to Congress dated August 18, President Obama announced that he was expanding the scope of the air campaign in Iraq to include the protection of key

Iraqi infrastructure and to pursue Islamic State forces wherever they might be in Iraq.[107]

On October 11, a force of approximately 10,000 IS troops from Mosul and Syria advanced toward Baghdad. By October 12, they had penetrated to within 15 miles of the Baghdad airport. In response, the US dispatched Apache Attack Helicopters to attack the advancing IS troops.[108] This was the first time the US military, other than for air forces, was directly engaged in conjunction with Iraqi troops against IS militants. On December 14, reportedly, US ground forces in conjunction with Iraqi Army units and Sunni militias clashed with IS militants near the Ein al-Assad base about 100 miles west of Baghdad in Anbar province. The base houses about 350 American advisers. The Pentagon subsequently denied that US ground troops had been involved in the attack.[109]

By the end of the year the US had conducted a total of 799 air strikes in Iraq and 572 in Syria at a total cost in excess of 1.1 billion dollars. Roughly 82 percent of all of the air strikes had been conducted by American air forces. The balance of the attacks in Iraq had been carried out by a combination of air forces from Belgium, Canada, France, the Netherlands, Australia, and the United Kingdom. While the balance of the attacks in Syria had been carried out by air forces from Saudi Arabia, Qatar, Jordan, Bahrain, Morocco, and the UAE. In addition, Italy and Spain offered aerial refueling and other support. Italy also offered four Panavia Tornado IDS fighter-bombers, but as of year-end it was not clear if these had actually been deployed in theater.

American military operations in the Syrian Civil War began on July 4, 2014, when, following US air strikes against an Islamic State base known as the Osama bin Laden Camp, two dozen US special forces parachuted in from helicopters. The mission was to capture potential high value IS personnel stationed at the camp as well as the freeing of Western hostages being held there. The US troops were also, it's believed, supported by Jordanian Special Forces personnel, although this has never been confirmed. The mission failed as the hostages had been moved the day before and no high value IS militants were found. Following a three hour firefight, US forces withdrew. In the month following the rescue attempt, American journalist James Foley, American aid worker Peter Kassig, and British aid workers David Haines and Alan Henning, were all beheaded by IS militants.

On August 26, the US began surveillance flights over Syria to gather intelligence on potential IS targets. The United States and its Arab allies began air strikes in Syria on September 22. The US also launched Tomahawk missiles from American ships in the eastern Mediterranean. According to Iranian sources, the White House assured Iran that it would only be targeting Islamic State and other radical jihadist groups affiliated with al-Qaeda, like the al-Nusra Front and the Khorasan Group, and that it did not intend to attack Syrian military forces.[110] Between September 22 and December 26, the United States along with air forces from Saudi Arabia, Jordan, Qatar, the UAE, Morocco, and Bahrain, conducted a total of 66 rounds of air strikes consisting of 572 missions. The United States did not officially ask the Syrian government for permission to intervene prior to its air attacks. It did, however, inform Syria's representative at the United Nations of intended air strikes; although not of the specific targets. To date, Syrian military radar and air defense systems have been "passive" during the American led air raids.[111]

Postscript: The Enemy of My Enemy is ...

The internationalization of the civil wars in Iraq and Syria, and their subsequent linkage, has created an exceedingly complex political environment. First, the role of the Syrian Civil War as a Sunni-Shia proxy contest that pitted Turkey, Saudi Arabia, and various Gulf States on one side, and Iran and its allies on the other, and has resulted in the provision of approximately 30 billion dollars of financial and military aid to the various antagonists. The result of this continued support has been to prolong the fighting and its resulting casualties and devastation far beyond what any of the antagonists would have been able to sustain on their own. It has also led to the *de facto* dissolution of the Syrian state. Syria today is less a nation than it is a collection of warlords and their petty fiefdoms. Assad, his support from Iran notwithstanding, has become little more than just another one, albeit the largest, of those warlords.

Moreover, notwithstanding the enormous amount of aid that the various antagonists has received, neither side has been successful in tipping the balance of the conflict. In the long term, Islamic State militants, lacking a reliable supplier of arms and heavy weaponry and limited to whatever they capture on the battlefield, will increasingly find themselves at a disadvantage in their struggle with both the armed forces of Iraq and Syria, as well as those of the other militant groups. Over time, the United States and its various allies will succeed in "degrading" Islamic State's capabilities, but this will not end the civil war in Syria and neither will it, in all probability, end the political instability in Iraq. The war with the Islamic State is merely the first round of what will likely be a long and protracted conflict for control of Syria.

Today there are five major, distinct antagonists in the Syrian civil war: the Assad government; the generally secular Free Syrian Army; Islamic State; the al-Qaeda affiliated jihadist groups, like the al-Nusra Front and the Khorasan Group; and the jihadist groups that are neither affiliated with al-Qaeda nor IS. The latter groups, notwithstanding the broad coalitions that they have been induced to join by the promise of more aid, do not share any consensus for what a post-Assad Syria should be like, both politically and socially. Fundamentally these groups are the most opportunistic and are likely to switch allegiances as circumstances warrant.

At the moment there is a tenuous consensus to focus on destroying Islamic State's capabilities to wage war and to roll back its territorial conquests. In Syria, American and various Arab air forces have intervened in support of the anti-IS coalition and their combined forces has been sufficient to stop the further expansion of the Islamic State's territory and even to roll back some of its conquests. There is little consensus on what comes next should the "anti-Islamic State" coalition succeed in degrading Islamic State's capabilities to such an extent that it is no longer a proto-nation state but goes back to being just another militant group. Turkey, Saudi Arabia, and their allies are committed to seeing the overthrow of the Assad regime. Washington is less certain now about the desirability of seeing Assad replaced. Will America's Arab partners continue their military intervention if the US withdraws from the Syrian Civil War? Certainly those countries do not have the capability of orchestrating as extensive an air campaign. Exactly how broad an air campaign they could carry out and whether they would do so on their own, remains to be seen.

The domestic stability of Iraq is now inexorably linked with the outcome of the Syrian Civil War. Sunni militants in Syria will invariably look for support and refuge within the Sunni community in Iraq. In turn, the more disenfranchised that community feels the more willing it will be to use both the presence of those militant groups, as well as its willingness to support them, as a source of leverage with the government in Baghdad. It is highly unlikely that the Iraqi government can succeed in securing its frontiers with Syria and pacifying western Iraq without the support and involvement of Iraq's Sunni community. As long as violence persists in Syria, and as long as Iraq's Sunni community feels it is being marginalized, it is going to be very difficult to prevent jihadist militants in

Syria from moving back and forth across the Syrian-Iraqi border and the accompanying violence from spilling over into Iraq.

There is also the larger issue of how the United States fits into the Sunni-Shia rivalry and the role of the Syrian Civil War as a proxy for this larger conflict. At the moment the air campaign against Islamic State effectively consists of two separate coalitions: an American-Arab one attacking IS in Syria and a coalition made up of the United States and various Western allies fighting IS in Iraq. To date, America's European allies have been unwilling to intervene in the Syrian Civil War by attacking Islamic State militants there. In light of a possible Islamic State connection with the terrorist attacks in Paris on January 9 and 10, this position, especially that of France, may change. At the same time Arab air forces have been unwilling to attack IS militants operating in Iraq. It is highly unlikely that Sunni Arab air forces are going to intervene in defense of a Shiite government in Iraq against either Islamic State or, what are likely to be, other Sunni, anti-Baghdad, militants.

The situation is made even more complicated by the fact that the Baghdad government is committed to preserving the Assad government in Damascus. Even if Iraq's Shiite government can do little to help the Assad regime, it certainly has shown that it will not prevent the transit of Iranian aid and military forces across Iraq. Baghdad and its Arab neighbors may be on the same side when it comes to battling Islamic State, but when it comes to dealing with the Assad regime and the Syrian Civil War; they are decidedly on opposite sides. The United States thus finds itself simultaneously on opposite sides of the Sunni-Shia rivalry: committed to maintaining a Shia government in Baghdad, albeit one that it hopes is more inclusive of the Sunni minority, while at the same time avoiding committing itself, as its Arab allies and Turkey have pushed it to do, to overthrowing the Assad government.

The role of Iran and its military forces in stabilizing Iraq and halting the Islamic State's advance adds an additional dimension of complexity to American policy deliberations. It's possible that the combination of the Islamic State's inability to properly administer its territories, domestic opposition to its violence and terror, not to mention the harshness of the Sharia laws that it wants to impose, and the degradation of its military capabilities will ultimately lead to the collapse of Islamic State. That's certainly possible. In the short term, however, as long as defending the Baghdad government from further incursions by IS militants requires "boots on the ground," then the stability of Iraq will be linked to the broader issue of American-Iranian relations. It is highly unlikely that any significant number of US ground troops will be reintroduced into Iraq. Politically, that is simply not an option that the Obama administration is willing to consider. It is even more unlikely that any of America's European or Arab allies are prepared to commit ground troops to fight against IS militants, or any other jihadist militants for that matter, in Iraq. The "boots on the ground," to the extent they are needed, will in all likelihood be Iranian and those of its Shia allies.

Tehran and Washington have common ground in defeating Islamic State, but all of the other issues that have divided the two governments remain. To a certain extent, Iraq's domestic stability has always been a factor in American-Iranian relations. Iran's ability to manipulate the Shia militias and its influence among Shia politicians and their political parties has played a role ever since the fall of Saddam Hussein. Moreover, a stable Shia dominated government in Baghdad is in Tehran's interest as well. Iran has ample reason to intervene in Iraq to support the Iraqi government regardless of its bearing on American-Iranian relations. What is unclear, at this point, is what the long-term consequences, if any, of this short term rapprochement may be. Will common ground in defending Baghdad lead to a long term thaw between the US and Iran or will it simply be a short term marriage of convenience like that which existed when the US attacked the Taliban government in Afghanistan?

Will the US soften its opposition to Iran's nuclear development program and the sanctions that have been imposed on Iran in return for Tehran's assistance in stabilizing Iraq? Will an agreement on Iran's nuclear program end up becoming a part of a larger American-Iranian agreement over the political future of the Middle East. The White House's urgency in coming to an agreement on Iran's nuclear development program may be driven simply by the desire to have a "foreign policy success" for an administration that has had few such "successes" or it may reflect the concern that Washington's negotiating position may grow weaker as the situation in Iraq and Syria persists. It is hard to escape the conclusion that Washington's reluctance to commit itself to the overthrow of the Assad regime is, if not a *quid pro quo* for Iranian assistance in Iraq, at the very least, shaped, unofficially, by that consideration. Moreover, both governments have a different view on what constitutes "stability" in Iraq. For the United States, long-term political stability requires a meaningful Sunni role in Iraqi politics and an end to the disenfranchisement and marginalization of the Sunni community there. For Iran, on the other hand, Sunni unrest, as long as it is kept within tolerable limits, ensures Baghdad's continued dependence on Tehran. What is inescapable is that the current campaign to degrade and roll back the Islamic State is simply the first act in what is going to be an extremely complex drama.

Chapter 5

Prelude to Collapse: Iraq, January 2012-May 2014

The speed with which ISIL forces took over western Iraq was astonishing. Within a matter of 90 days, or so, an area covering approximately 50,000 square miles fell under the control of ISIL.[112] "Control," however, is a term that has to be used rather loosely here. It would be correct to say that within 90 days, ISIL found itself in a position where it could project its military force over a region of roughly 50,000 square miles with limited opposition from the Iraqi government in Baghdad. While that may not be quite the same as "control" it does come awfully close to it. In reality, notwithstanding the fact that its success was quite astounding, large portions of this area were already under the *de facto* control of ISIL before the start of the June 2014 offensive.

The Awakening Movement and the organization of the Sunni militias had not resulted in the destruction of ISI, but it did succeed in significantly degrading its capabilities. What the Awakening Movement did accomplish was to isolate ISI from the rest of the Sunni community in the Sunni dominated regions of Iraq. Simply put, it deprived it of a significant base of support while simultaneously offering protection to those elements in the community that were willingly to publically oppose it. The withdrawal of US troops from Iraq in 2011 eliminated an important element of support for the Awakening Movement. The Baghdad's government unwillingness to carry out its promises to the Sunni community, coupled with continued attempts to marginalize the Sunnis in Iraq, would allow ISI and other jihadist groups to reestablish the position they had held at the height of the first Iraqi insurgency.

The Second Iraqi Insurgency: January 2012-May 2014

In January 2012, ISI took responsibility for a string of bombings in Baghdad, Nasiriya, and Basra.[113] This was followed by a series of attacks, on February 23, across fifteen Iraqi cities that left more than 250 injured and 83 dead. Once again ISI took responsibility. On March 5, a group of ISI militants disguised in Iraqi military uniforms attacked and killed 27 policemen and then raised the flag of al-Qaeda. Additional attacks followed.

On March 20 a wave of attacks in Baghdad and Karbala left 52 dead and 250 injured. Another wave of bombs, this time more than 20, exploded across Iraq on April 19, leaving 36 dead and 170 wounded. On June 4, a suicide bomber killed 26 people and injured around 200 at the offices of a Shiite foundation in Baghdad. Another series of attacks occurred on June 13, which left 93 people dead and over 300 injured. In each case, ISI took responsibility for the bombings.

The pattern of attacks continued over the summer and autumn of 2012. On July 3, attacks occurred in Diwaniyah, Karbala, Taji, and Tuz Khormato resulting in the deaths of 40 people and injuries to an additional 122 others. On July 23, car bombs in Baghdad, Najaf, and Mahmoudiyah killed 23 and wounded another 74. On June 23, another string of attacks across Iraq killed 116 and left 299 injured. On July 31, another series of attacks, this time twin car bombings in Baghdad, killed 24 and injured 61. On August 13, in the bloodiest attack since 2009, another series of attacks across Iraq left 128 dead and more than 400 injured. More attacks followed on Sept 9, 108 killed and 370 injured, and again on September 30, 37 dead and 90 injured. On October 27, during the Eid al-Adha holidays, another sting of bombings in Baghdad, Mosul, Taji, and Muqdadiya, left 46 dead and 123 injured. Another car bombing in Baghdad, on October 28, left 15 dead and 33 injured. On November 6, a suicide bombing outside of an Iraqi Army base in Taji resulted in the death of 31 soldiers and recruits, and injuries to 50 others. On November 14, another string of deadly bombings left 29 dead and 194 injured and, on November 27, a string of eight car bombings across Iraq left 29 dead and 128 wounded. Once again, ISI took responsibility for the attacks, although in some cases other organizations also claimed credit.

The pattern of attacks was similar to the early phase of the insurgency in 2004. Attacks, mostly in the form of suicide bombers, were directed at Shia civilians and police stations and army bases. The one difference was that none of the attacks occurred in Anbar province and in particular in either Fallujah or Ramadi. Despite the heightened insurgency and the deaths of over 4,600 people, Anbar province remained generally quiet. Moreover, ISI still lacked the strength to directly challenge government forces. The death toll in 2012 marked the first time since 2009 that the death toll had increased after two years of decline. The end of 2012 also saw the beginning of the Sunni "Arab Spring" inspired demonstrations. The specific catalyst had been the ongoing standoff between Prime Minister al-Maliki and Vice President al-Hashimi and the harassment of Sunni Finance Minister Rafi al-Issawi.[114] On December 23, in Fallujah, thousands of Sunni marched in protests against the Baghdad government.

The pattern of violence continued into 2013, but now it was also entwined with a rising tide of Sunni protest. Moreover, in addition to attacks against Shia civilians, ISI now began to target police and military units in the Sunni triangle as well. In January a series of bombings targeted Shiite pilgrims in Musayyib and Karbala resulting in 28 deaths and 60 injuries. A suicide bomber in Fallujah killed Sunni MP Sadoun al-Essawi, a prominent member of the Sons of Iraq committee. On January 16, a suicide bomber exploded a truck bomb outside the offices of the Kurdistan Democratic Party (KDP) in Kirkuk resulting in 26 deaths and 204 injuries. A similar attack against KDP offices in Tuz Khormato killed five and wounded another 40. Roadside bombings across Iraq in the middle of the month left an additional 24 dead and 44 injured. Additional attacks, in and around Baghdad on January 22, resulted in 26 dead and 58 injured. The next day a suicide bomber detonated a bomb during a funeral in Tuz Khormato killing 42 and injuring another 75. In the meantime, the ongoing protests against the Maliki government had turned deadly. On January 23, in Fallujah, soldiers opened fire against demonstrators throwing rocks at them resulting in the deaths of seven protestors and injuries to 70 more. In retaliation, militants shot three soldiers.

On February 3, a suicide bomber dressed as a policeman and driving a police car detonated a car bomb near the provincial police headquarters in Kirkuk. The attack killed 36 people and injured 105 more. Among the injured was Major General Jamal Tahir, Kirkuk's Chief of Police. Concurrently with the attack, three militant gunmen attacked, security forces responding to the blast, with grenades. On March 19, the tenth anniversary of the start of the Iraqi war, a series of bombings across Iraq killed 98 and injured 240 more. A bomb-laden tanker was exploded, on April 1, at the Tikrit Police Headquarters, killing 42 people and injuring 67 others. The attack was followed by another series of bombings across more than 20 Iraqi cities resulting in 75 fatalities and 350 injuries.

On April 23, Iraqi Army units moved against an encampment set up by Sunni demonstrators in the town of Hawija.[115] The Iraqi government believed that Sunni militants from the Naqshbandi Army were organizing the protestors. The clash quickly turned deadly, resulting in 42 deaths and 153 injuries. The "Hawija clashes" also sparked a new round of demonstrations and revenge attacks. Naqshbandi Army militants captured the town of Sulaiman Bek, 100 miles north of Baghdad. In what was to become a familiar pattern, they withdrew the next day and escaped with weapons and military vehicles. More than 340 people were killed and 600 injured in the wave of violence that followed the Hawija clashes. Over 700 people, including 112 members of the Iraqi military, were killed in April. This was the highest death toll since June 2008. The violence continued to mount over the months of May and June. A week of deadly bombings over northern and central Iraq, during the middle of May, resulted in 449 deaths and another 732 injuries.

That same month the Iraqi military launched Operation al-Shabah, "Phantom." The operation was both in response to Baghdadi's announcement that Jabhat al-Nusra was an extension of AQI in Iraq and that the two groups were merging to form the Islamic State of Iraq and al-Sham (ISIS), as well as the mounting pattern of coordination between the two groups, especially in western Anbar province. In collaboration with Syrian military units, the goal was to get better control of the border area between Iraq and Syria and sever the link between al-Nusra and AQI, as well as to prevent the movement of arms and militants from Syria to Iraq. Both Iraqi and Syrian border stations were often coming under fire from militants in both countries. In one instance, Syrian border guards had crossed into Iraq to escape their attackers. As they were being returned by Iraqi troops to Syria, on March 4, the convoy carrying them was ambushed at Akashat, leaving 51 Syrian soldiers and 13 Iraqi soldiers dead.

The operation began on May 20 and continued until mid-July. Several hundred militants were killed and a number of arms caches and safe houses were destroyed. The Iraqi military claimed that it had captured large stocks of weapons, which it claimed were "Turkish made." Operation al-Shabah was deemed a success by the Iraqi government. It was significant because it underscored the fact that the Syrian and Iraqi insurgencies were increasingly linked, and by the fact that Baghdad and Damascus were now openly working together, especially in western areas of Anbar and Nineveh provinces, to secure the area from militants. From a practical standpoint, little changed. Once the Iraqi Army withdrew, the attacks against border posts continued and the smuggling of weapons and militants across the border resumed.

The bomb attacks continued into the summer. In early June, a string of bombings struck central and northern Iraq leaving 94 people dead and injuring more than 300. A second series of bombings, these ones mostly in the south, left 54 people dead and more than 170 injured. Bomb attacks continued to rise over the summer and autumn of 2013. Not only did the pace of attacks increase but increasingly, in a prelude to open warfare, they were being directed at government offices and against military and police units. Many attacks were centered in Baghdad. Shia neighborhoods, in particular, were being targeted in response to what ISIS called the systematic terrorization and expulsion of Sunni inhabitants in Baghdad by Shia militias. In September a total of 979 people were killed and 2,138 were wounded. Deaths in October were also 979, although injuries dropped slightly to 1,902. Roughly half of the casualties occurred in Baghdad and the region surrounding it.

The death toll in November was 948, of which 852 were civilians, 53 were police officers, and 43 were Iraqi Army soldiers. December saw the biggest increase in violence since the peak of the previous insurgency with suicide bombs and militant attacks occurring virtually every day. Another 759 people were killed in the month of December, 661 civilians and 98 from the police and military, and another 1,345 were wounded. For the year, casualties were approximately 9,000 killed, 7,818 civilians and 1,050 security personnel, and over 20,000 were injured. These casualty figures were the highest since 2008 and were almost double the casualties in 2012.

There were a larger number of organizations "tracking" the casualty figures in Iraq and their numbers rarely agreed. What is clear, is that the NGO's tracking the casualties always had numbers that were significantly higher than those published by the Iraqi government in Baghdad. Regardless of whose figures were used, however, all of the various sets of statistics were consistent when it came to the trend line—the casualties were going up as the violence steadily mounted and Iraq slipped again into a full scale insurgency and a *de facto* civil war.

As 2013 came to a close, ISIS claimed it had taken control of large parts of Mosul. On January 4, 2014, after several days of fighting, ISIS claimed it had "captured" Fallujah, both reports were denied by the government in Baghdad. Both sides in the conflict use the terms "control" and "capture" rather loosely. It's important to understand both how the terms are used and how they fit into the broader pattern of the conflict. After the withdrawal of American troops from Iraq in 2011, the various jihadist groups, primarily ISI, responded with a strategy of random suicide bombings. These were "random" in the sense that, although the specific targets may have been carefully chosen, they were primarily targets of opportunity. They were not part of a broader military strategy designed to accomplish a specific military objective. There was no follow-up to the attack, nor was the attack part of a larger military operation. This was similar to the pattern of the insurgency from June 2003 through most of 2004.

As ISI's strength increased, and as the Baghdad government lost support among the Sunni communities in Iraq, the presence of the jihadists became more visible. Suicide bombings would at times be followed by additional attacks by gunmen designed to target remaining survivors or first respondents among the military and police. As 2013 progressed, ISI was increasingly willing to demonstrate its "power" by setting up manned checkpoints, engaging in fire fights with Iraqi security forces, and later in "extended battles" with Iraqi military forces that might last for several days. Then, starting in late 2013, and increasingly over the first half of 2014, ISIS would announce that it had taken "control" of specific towns or cities. This was more or less the pattern of the Iraqi insurgency from 2004 through 2007, before the organization of the Awakening Councils and the US "surge" began to reduce the power of jihadists.

In this context "control" often described the visibility of ISIS forces within Sunni areas/neighborhoods that were willing, or had been intimidated, to accept their presence. This "visibility" often took the form of coexistence between the Baghdad or provincial governments and ISIS. Jihadists might man checkpoints, while Iraqi police forces were still technically in control of the area. If challenged by police, jihadists might simply melt away and return after the police had passed. Alternatively, depending on how strong they felt, they might challenge any police show of force and a gun battle might erupt. The Iraqi police might opt to challenge the outward manifestation of jihadist power or they might choose to simply ignore their activity and remain in the relative safety of their police station.

Once ISIS had obtained "control" of an area they might take responsibility for some social services, often times these would run in parallel with similar programs administered by the Iraqi government. ISIS might levy its own "jihadi taxes," effectively a shakedown, of local businesses. The curriculum of local schools might be altered to reflect the beliefs of ISIS, but often times, salaries would continue to be paid by the central government. Even now, both the Syrian and Iraqi governments are continuing to pay the salaries of some civil servants in areas that are part of the Islamic State. Non-Sunni inhabitants might be intimidated into leaving. Community leaders, journalists, and other influential individuals would be targeted for assassination unless they agreed to support ISIS, but otherwise the pace of daily life would seem unchanged.

In this sense, "control" meant the ability of ISIS to project enough military force to deter the Iraqi government from trying to exert enough countervailing force to compel ISIS jihadists to leave or risk being killed. Through early 2014, as during the period from 2003 through 2008, the Iraqi government and US forces had possessed the ability to bring enough military power to bear to force the jihadists to either leave of face annihilation.

The constraint was not the inability to project that power, but the civilian casualties that would have resulted from that conflict and the long-term consequences of those casualties for both jihadist support and recruitment, along with the long-term stability of those areas. What happened after June 2014 is that the collapse of the Iraqi Army meant that Baghdad, to a large extent, lost the ability to project any kind of sufficient countervailing force in those areas "controlled" by Islamic State, regardless of whether it was willing to tolerate the civilian casualties that would have resulted.

The beginning of 2014 saw a significant internationalization of the conflict between ISIS and the other jihadist groups. On January 4, ISIS took responsibility for a car bomb that exploded in the Beirut suburb of Haret Hreik, the neighborhood that hosts the headquarters of Hezbollah.[116] Four people were killed and seventy seven were wounded in the attack. This was followed by an announcement, on January 25, that ISIS was creating a new Lebanese arm to fight the Shia militant group Hezbollah in Lebanon.[117] At the same time there were reports that ISIS was looking to organize cells in Afghanistan.[118] In the meantime, at the urging of Western and especially Arab aid donors, many of the rebel groups announced alliances targeting ISIS. On January 3, the FSA, the Islamic Front, and the newly organized Army of Mujahedeen, announced they would cooperate in an offensive against ISIS in the Syrian provinces of Aleppo and Idlib. The Army of Mujahedeen was a coalition of Islamist rebel groups consisting of Division 19, Fastaquim Kama Umirt (Be Upright as Ordered), and the Nour al-Din al-Zenki (Light of the Faith Islamic Brigades), as well as a number of other groups. The groups had been receiving funding and arms from various Arab governments in the Gulf and had formed the coalition at their urging.

On January 6, a coalition of Syrian rebel groups managed to expel ISIS forces from Ar-Raqqah, (Raqqa) the de facto capital of ISIS.[119] Two days later, a coalition of rebel groups expelled ISIS forces from Aleppo. In the meantime, ISIS forces in Anbar province captured al-Karmah, Hit, al-Khalidiya, Haditha, and the city and border crossing at Al Qaim. Fighting also raged in Ramadi and Abu Ghraib. By the end of the month ISIS forces had recaptured Ar-Raqqah, but their attempt to retake Aleppo failed and they lost control of additional villages west of the city.

In February al-Nusra Front announced that it was joining the other Syrian rebel groups in opposing ISIS. By mid-February they had succeeded in expelling ISIS forces from Deir ez-Zor province in the eastern part of Syria. On February 3, al-Qaeda announced that it was formally terminating its relationship with ISIS and that it would devote its energy to working with the other jihadist groups to overthrow the Assad government in Syria.[120] In Iraq, on March 16, Baghdad announced that Iraqi forces had retaken Ramadi and parts of Fallujah. In Syria, ISIS consolidated its forces around Ar-Raqqah in anticipation of a new offensive in Syria. In response to an attack staged by an ISIS cell in Turkey, on March 20, the Turkish government announced that it would crack down on ISIS cells in Turkey and launched a series of raids on Istanbul leading to the arrest of several ISIS members.[121]

Open warfare continued over the months of April and May. While the pattern of suicide bombings continued in Iraq, ISIS in Syria, found itself under attack from both other jihadist groups and the Syrian military. In Iraq, on the other hand, there was little resistance from other jihadist groups. Many of them were in fact now working with ISIS. The Iraqi insurgency had now morphed into a civil war between ISIS and the Iraqi military supported by remnants of some of the Sunni militias. Between May 9 and 18, the Iraqi Army retook sixteen villages around Fallujah. As the fighting in Syria with other jihadist groups intensified, ISIS militants began to subject Muslim opponents to beheadings and public crucifixions.[122] Initially victims were shot before being crucified but there were unconfirmed reports of actual crucifixions in Ar-Raqqah. Notwithstanding their Christian symbolism, the victims of the crucifixions were all Muslims. The terror campaign would move into high gear when ISIS militants would, in June, launch an all-out invasion of Iraq.

Postscript: The Iraqi Insurgency Take 2

The period between January 2012 and May 2014 is notable for three significant developments. The first was a return of a broad-based insurgency against the government in Baghdad. Just as in the first insurgency (2003-2008), it began with a random pattern of opportunistic acts of violence against Shia civilians as well as Iraqi military and police forces. The tempo of attacks steadily increased until casualties reached the levels of the previous insurgency. As before, car bombs began to be accompanied by follow-up attacks against survivors and first responders. Jihadist militants became increasingly more visible and openly challenged police forces in the cities of the Sunni Triangle. Gunfights between ISIS militants steadily escalated from short skirmishes to drawn out battles, and by the beginning of 2014, into open civil war.

The second development was the attempt by ISIS to take control of the jihadist militants in the Syrian Civil War in much the same way as it had taken control of the earlier insurgency in Iraq. Their effort had a mixed success. On the one hand, ISIS was successful in recruiting a significant number of jihadists from other organizations and by the end of 2013 had emerged as one of the largest of the jihadist organizations operating in Syria. Ignoring the various "coalitions" that had been formed among the jihadist groups in Syria, which in theory seemed to have more militants, they were the largest. On the other hand, a significant number of jihadist organizations and their militants declined to accept ISIS's leadership and eventually found themselves in open conflict with ISIS. The battle between ISIS and its jihadist opponents would prove to be as bloody and as ferocious as the battle being fought with Assad's military forces. ISIS's gambit also led to an irrevocable break with al-Qaeda and the two organizations quickly found themselves in open competition for the leadership of the international jihadist movement.

Finally, ISIS's role in Syria would link together the Syrian Civil war and the *de facto* civil war in Iraq. Eventually, as ISIS carved out for itself a new state straddling both Syria and Iraq and declared the creation of Islamic State as a worldwide caliphate, it found itself simultaneously at war with both the Syrian and Iraqi governments and their allies. The linkage of the two conflicts would in turn produce a broad, though in part unofficial, coalition committed to degrading the military power of IS and eventually stripping it of its territorial domain. While that coalition might have a tenuous agreement on the need to degrade Islamic State, it agreed on little else. Should it succeed in eventually destroying or severely weakening IS, the members of the anti-IS coalition will quickly find themselves on opposing sides of the next conflict over the future of the Assad government in Syria and the best way of ensuring the stability of the Baghdad government.

Moreover, notwithstanding the dramatic success that ISIS and subsequently Islamic State would achieve in overrunning large areas of western and central Iraq in the summer of 2014, large areas of the Sunni Triangle and its principal cities were effectively under its control long before the invasion in June 2014. The failure of the al-Maliki government to follow through on promises made to the Awakening Councils and the Sunni Militias, plus the continuing attempts to marginalize the Sunni Community in Iraq, would set the stage for a renewal of the insurgency that had been brought under control in 2009. At the same time, the militants IS recruited in Syria, plus the weaponry that it was able to capture or secure there, would significantly enhance its offensive capabilities and lead, not only to its success on the battlefield against Iraqi government forces, but to its eventual transformation from a militant jihadist organization into a proto-nation state.

Chapter 6

ISIS Triumphant: The Iraqi Civil War, June 2014-January 2015

On June 5, 2014, ISIS began a major offensive against Iraqi government forces in western Iraq. That same day ISIS militants captured large parts of the city of Samarra. They advanced to within a mile of the al-Askari Mosque, one of the holiest sites of Shia Muslims, in the center of the city, before the arrival of fresh troops pushed them out of Samara. While seemingly a defeat, the advance and subsequent retreat from Samara had allowed ISIS militants to withdraw with large quantities of captured weaponry. This pattern would be repeated throughout the summer of 2014, until the collapse of Iraqi forces made these tactical retreats unnecessary.

The next day, June 6, ISIS forces attacked Mosul and captured the western part of the city. ISIS forces were estimated at approximately 1,500 to 3,000 militants, although they received help from ISIS cells inside Mosul. Approximately 15,000 Iraqi soldiers opposed them. In addition, ISIS received assistance from a number of other militant groups. Two in particular are worth noting as they underscore the complexity and fluidity of the changing alliances that made ISIS's success possible. These two organizations, both Ba'athist inspired militant groups, were: Jaysh Rijal at-Tariqa an-Naqshabandiya (Army of the Men of Naqshbandi Order) or Naqshbandi Army (NA) and al-Majlis al-'Askari al-Amm li-Thuwwar al-'Iraq (The General Military Council for Iraqi Revolutionaries, GMCIR).

The Naqshbandi has also been referred to as the Supreme Council for Jihad and Liberation. The Naqshbandi Army was a militant group of former Ba'athist party members led by Izzat Ibrahim al-Douri, a former Iraqi vice-president under Saddam Hussein and deputy chairman of the Revolutionary Command Council. The group has had several names and at times appears to have used multiple names simultaneously. Al-Douri is also the leader of the "New Ba'ath" party. The NA was originally organized in 2003 as part of the Ba'athist inspired militancy. After the death of Hussein, it evolved into one of a number of Sufi inspired, Ba'ath militant insurgency groups. Naqshbandi refers to one of the major spiritual orders of Sufism, an Islamic sect. It is the only order that traces its spiritual lineage directly to the prophet Muhammad and as such can be characterized as a common ground between Sunnis and Sufis. The association with Sufism is, nonetheless, confusing as Sufism is characterized by a non-violent philosophy. Moreover, militant Sunni jihadists consider Sufis apostates and have typically targeted them.

The MCIR, on the other hand, is an organization comprised of former Ba'athist political and military leaders. The council was organized in 2013 to unify Sunni "Arab Spring" protestors as well as former members of the Sunni militias. The MCIR claims that it is "a professional army"[123] and that it adheres to the Geneva Convention for the treatment of prisoners. It also claims to be a secular organization, although its membership is predominantly Sunni, and that it is seeking a "democratic solution" to the crisis in Iraq.[124]

MCIR forces cooperated with ISIS in the attack on Mosul. Following the capture of the city, a member of MCIR, a former Ba'athist major general named Azhar al-Ubaidi, was appointed the governor of Mosul. Ahmed Abdul Rashid, another former Ba'athist general was appointed governor of Tikrit when that city was taken. The cooperation between organizations like MCIR and NA with ISIS underscore the "alliances of convenience" that characterize the current political situation in Syria and Iraq. Notwithstanding the fact that their underlying ideologies are completely incompatible, both MCIR and NA have received funding from ISIS and have used ISIS suicide bombers to attack their opponents. In return they have provided military and administrative support to ISIS.

At the other extreme from ISIS, MCIR also has strong links to the Hayat al-Ulama al-Muslimin (Association of Muslim Scholars, AMS). The AMS is a group of Sunni religious leaders that was organized on April 14, 2003. Its primary function has been to administer a charitable fund for the maintenance of religious buildings. It has exerted significant political influence however. It strongly opposed the American led invasion and subsequent occupation and called for a boycott of elections until the US agreed to a date for the withdrawal of all foreign troops in Iraq. The association gave religious sanction to the Sunni insurgency but, at the same time, they have consistently condemned acts of terrorist violence against civilians. The AMS denounced Zarqawi's call "for a full scale war on Shiites" and claimed that such actions were "not justified by Islamic law." The association has also sponsored joint Sunni-Shia prayer sessions as part of its attempts to heal the sectarian divisions within Iraq.[125]

As ISIS forces advanced into Mosul they unleashed a terror campaign against Iraqi Army soldiers. Although not all of the reports have been verified, and it is unclear how many soldiers were killed, there were numerous accounts of Iraqi soldiers being hanged, set ablaze, or crucified by ISIS militants.[126] Simultaneously with the ISIS advance, ISIS cells within

Mosul, aided by significant elements of the local population, sprang up and began to attack Iraqi police and military units. These attacks at the rear of the Iraqi defensive lines further complicated the battle and gave rise to numerous, false reports, that ISIS forces had broken through the Iraqi lines and prompted Iraqi retreats. Iraqi forces began to withdraw from Mosul on June 9. The withdrawal, poorly executed, triggered mass defections and desertions from the Iraqi soldiers remaining in Mosul. Police units in the city continued to fight, even after the withdrawal of the Iraqi military, until they too were overwhelmed. On June 10, ISIS forces captured the Mosul airport including Iraqi military helicopters and jet fighters, as well as the main prison complex and Mosul Police Headquarters. By the end of the day, all resistance in Mosul had ended and ISIS was in control of the city.

In the meantime, as ISIS forces began to advance on Route 80 towards Kirkuk, 100 miles to the southeast, Iraqi Army units abandoned the city. They left behind much of their heavy equipment, including a dozen tanks and a large number of Humvees and trucks. Taking advantage of the situation, the Peshmerga, the military forces of Iraqi Kurdistan, moved in and took control of Kirkuk.

On June 11, ISIS forces took control of Baiji, 130 miles north of Baghdad, the site of Iraq's largest oil refinery. Baiji was also a key transportation hub and lay astride Route 1, one of the major highways into Baghdad. That same evening, ISIS forces took Tikrit, a Ba'athist stronghold and the hometown of Saddam Hussein. Tikrit was also the location of a major Iraqi military base, the former American base Camp Speicher, as well as the Tikrit South Air Base (formerly FOB Remagen). Simultaneously, ISIS forces renewed their attack on Samara, only 80 miles from Baghdad. By June 12, ISIS militants had taken control of portions of Udhaim on the shores of Lake Dam, east of Tikrit and just 60 miles from Baghdad. On June 13, ISIS captured Saadiyah and Jalawla in Diyala Province.

In the meantime, an Iraqi Border Patrol Battalion, stationed at Rabia on Highway 1, abandoned its position in the face of advancing ISIS troops. Rabia was one of only two border crossings between Syria and Iraq. The other border crossing at al-Qa'im was captured by the FSA and al-Nusra Front on June 17. On June 23, ISIS militants seized control of the Karameh/Turaibil border crossing, the only border station between Jordan and Iraq. At approximately the same time, they seized control of the two border stations linking Iraq and Saudi Arabia at Arar and Nukhayb. Following the loss of the Jordanian and Saudi border crossings there were unconfirmed reports that the Iraqi Army had abandoned those posts under direct order of Iraqi Prime

Minister Maliki and that the action was taken in order to prompt Saudi and Jordanian intervention against ISIS.[127] Iraqi military forces subsequently retook the Turaibil and al Rabia border crossings several weeks later. Their status as of January 2015 was unclear.[128] Both Jordanian and Saudi military forces along the border were reinforced following ISIS's takeover of the Iraqi side of the border posts, but no further action was taken. The Jordanian border crossing continues to operate while the Saudi border crossings have been temporarily closed.

Between June 15 and 28, the Iraqi Army launched a series of counteroffensives against ISIS forces in Samara, al-Dhuluiya, and al-Mutasim. Significantly, the counteroffensive included elements of the Quds Force and Iranian Revolutionary Guard units. The Quds force is a special paramilitary force of Iran's Revolutionary Guard and is responsible for military operations outside of Iran. It's believed that the Quds Force operated in Afghanistan, both in support of Ahmad Shah Massoud's Northern Alliance against the Taliban and later with Taliban insurgents fighting the US and NATO backed force in the country. It is also suspected that they were involved in supporting Sunni Kurds fighting Saddam Hussein, and that they assisted Bosnian Muslims during the civil war in Bosnia. The Quds Force, along with Hezbollah, played a key role in the training of Muslim insurgents, both Shia and others, in Iraq during the insurgency.

In recent years the Quds Force has emerged as a key player in training fundamentalist Islamic terrorist groups. It also works closely with the Iranian government's Office of Liberation Movements. The office serves as a central clearinghouse and maintains contacts with underground Islamic militant organizations throughout the entire world.

Iran's Revolutionary Guards, or Army of the Guardians of the Islamic Revolution, is a branch of Iran's military. The purpose of the Revolutionary Guards is to protect the Islamic system and the Iranian Islamic Revolution. The Guards number some 125,000 personnel. They also control the Basji militia, a paramilitary volunteer militia, which number around 90,000 civilians. This was the first time that Iranian military units had participated openly with Iraqi Army units.[129] Notwithstanding Iraqi government claims that the counteroffensive pushed ISIS forces back, it does not appear that any substantial gains were made.

In the meantime, on June 15, insurgent forces consisting primarily of the Naqshbandi Army, and some elements of the MCIR, captured Tal Afar and its nearby air base. ISIS claimed that approximately 2,000 soldiers captured at Tal Afar had been executed. Only about 170 deaths, however, were actually confirmed.[130] The actual number of soldiers captured or executed remains unclear. Over the next several weeks ISIS forces continued to make inroads into Diyala and Anbar provinces and had surrounded, on three sides, the Balad Air Base (the former Camp Anaconda). The Iraqi military launched a second counteroffensive lasting from June 26 through July 21, directed at retaking Tikrit and obtaining control of the army base there (Camp Speicher). Once again, despite Iraqi Government's claims of success, there was little tangible change in the military situation. On June 29, ISIS announced that it was changing its name to Islamic State and proclaimed the existence of a worldwide caliphate.

At the beginning of August, IS militants moved against Kurdish positions in northern Iraq. On August 3, IS forces captured the town of Zumar and a nearby oil field. Concurrently, militants captured the town of Sinjar and, a few days later Qaraqosh, prompting an exodus of approximately 200,000 Christians and Yezidis. The Christians are members of the Chaldean Catholic Church, a branch of the Roman Catholic Church. One of the recent patriarchs of the Chaldean Church also served as a Roman Catholic cardinal. The Yezidis are a Kurdish sect that practice an ancient religion linked to Zoroastrianism, but which also embodies elements of Christianity.

Approximately 40,000 Yezidis were trapped on Sinjar Mountain and surrounded by IS militants. The Yezidis' plight, as well as mounting concern over the success of IS's campaign in Iraq and the Baghdad Government's inability to mount an effective counterattack, prompted the United States to begin air strikes, on August 7, against IS insurgents in Iraq. The US also began to directly supply arms to Kurdish fighters. The air campaign against IS was expanded into Syria beginning on September 22. The siege of Sinjar Mountain was initially broken on August 14, when Kurdish Peshmerga troops opened a corridor from Sinjar Mountain into Syria, and from there into Iraqi Kurdistan, allowing some 30,000 Yezidis to escape before IS forces closed off the corridor. The siege was finally broken on December 18, when Kurdish Peshmerga forces, accompanied by Yezidi militias (YKK), launched the Sinjar Offensive from Zumar and reopened a corridor to Mount Sinjar, allowing the remaining 10,000 Yezidis to escape to Iraqi Kurdistan.

Islamic State made some additional gains in Nineveh province, taking Tal Kaif on August 6, followed by, Bartella, and Karemlash. They also took the Mosul Dam and Makhmour, although Peshmerga forces, supported by US air power, later retook both sites.[131] After September 1, the ground situation largely stabilized. On October 14, IS forces captured the city of Hit. On October 24, Iraqi military units launched Operation Ashura. The operation aimed at retaking the strategic city of Jurf al Sakhar (the name has since been changed to Jurf a-Nasr or "Victory Bank"). The town, located roughly halfway between Baghdad and the holy city of Karbala and about 50 miles east of Fallujah, allowed IS militants to threaten attacks on Karbala during the Shia holy festival of Ashura. The town lies on a road taken by millions of Shia pilgrims traveling from Baghdad and the northeast to Karbala. The operation was successful. It was notable for the presence of Quds forces and one of its elite commanders, General Qasem Soleimani. Iraqi government sources denied that Iranian troops had been part of the attacking force or that Soleimani had been in command of the operation, although they later acknowledged that he had "planned the operation."[132]

A few weeks later, on October 29, Iraqi forces began an advance toward the city of Baiji. On November 7, Iraqi forces recaptured most of the city, including the oil refinery. IS militants withdrew completely on November 18, ceding control to the Iraqi government. An IS counterattack on December 21, however, restored to them control of the city. In the meantime, a Kurdish offensive recaptured Zumar on October 24, and on November 23 Jalawla, while Iraqi forces retook Sadiyah that same day. Kurdish forces entered Sinjar on December 20, and as 2014 drew to a close, were advancing east on Tal Afar, roughly half way between Sinjar and Mosul.

As 2015 began, the world's attention continued to be focused on the Kurdish town of Kobani. The town was in northern Syria abutting the Turkish border, but the battle to control it underscored how closely intertwined the civil wars in Iraq and Syria had become. On September 16, IS forces in Syria launched a broad offensive to capture the town of Kobani, and the villages surrounding it, and advance to the Syrian border with Turkey. By October 2, IS had succeeded in capturing 350 Kurdish villages in the area, creating over 300,000 Kurdish refugees, and had encircled Kobani on three sides and were beginning to advance into the town. According to unconfirmed reports from Kurdish refugees, IS militants were beheading any Kurdish fighters, both male and female, which they captured.

Starting on September 27, US and Arab coalition planes had begun targeted air strikes against IS positions around Kobani. They also began the aerial resupply of the troops in Kobani. In the meantime, Kurdish and Free Syrian Army troops in Kobani were being reinforced by additional FSA troops that were traveling there via Turkey. On October 31, after a protracted diplomatic negotiation, the Turkish government agreed to let Kurdish Peshmerga troops from Iraq cross into Kobani via Turkey. This was the first time that Ankara had allowed troops from outside Syria to reinforce the fighters defending Kobani. On November 5, the Kurdish Regional government "smuggled" several truckloads of ammunition across the Turkish border crossing for the fighters in Kobani. It's not clear if the Turkish government was aware of the shipment and simply chose to feign ignorance or whether they were in fact unaware.

IS forces attempted on at least four occasions to seize control of the Turkish border crossings and completely cut off Kobani, but were unable to do so. Beginning on November 1, Kurdish Peshmerga began a series of counterattacks against IS positions in the town. Control over the city was bitterly fought over during the months of November, December and January. As January drew to a close it appeared that Islamic State militants had been pushed out of most of the town but the situation remained fluid.

Postscript: Islamic State at the Tipping Point

The success of Islamic State in carving out for itself its own country has saddled it with three significant challenges. First, having created a nation, or at least, the outward appearance of one, it now has to figure out how to run it. If past history is a guide, there is little support for IS's social agenda within the Sunni community in Iraq. While Sunni in belief and culture, this is not a community that is instinctively jihadist in its orientation. Although in many ways traditional, there are elements of it that are also significantly secular and modernistic in its outlook. In short, jihadist militants like Islamic State have little in common with the Sunni community in Iraq. Ultimately its success in garnering long-term support will depend on its effectiveness in governing. Public administration and governance is not a skill set that Islamic State has in abundance. Significantly it has formed an alliance of convenience with former Ba'athist government and military officials and has relied on them for the administrative management of the larger cities under its control. Ideologically Islamic State and the Ba'athists have nothing in common, and their mutual support is at best transitory. It is based on the flimsiest foundation of mutual convenience imaginable. As 2015 began, there were already numerous reports of mounting tensions between Islamic State and its Ba'athist administrators, and rising complaints over the Islamic State's inability to reliably provide and finance essential public services.

Secondly, lacking a "sponsor," or a supplier of heavy military equipment, IS militants are dependent on what they can capture on the battlefield to replace damaged equipment and ammunition. As resistance stiffens and as its opponents began to roll it back, its opportunity to secure new arms on the battlefield, or from its captured opponents, will diminish significantly. Increasingly it will find itself at a disadvantage against its better-armed opponents. Unable to resist them on the open battlefield, it will be forced to slip back into the role of an insurgency, especially in the urban centers of the Sunni Triangle. If that occurs, then the situation will become increasingly like the first Iraqi insurgency during 2004-2008. The cities of the Sunni Triangle will became a no-man's land where the Iraqi government was unwilling to root out the jihadists for fear that civilian casualties would rebound in favor of the jihadists while the jihadists will lack the ability to hold any territory outside of the urban centers.

The third issue is that Islamic State's success had succeeded in pulling together a *de facto*, if unspoken, alliance of countries and groups that were usually at odds with one another. How else could one explain Iran, Saudi Arabia, the United States, Turkey, and organizations like Hamas, al-Qaeda, the Quds Force, and the Peshmerga, all sharing a common objective of degrading or destroying Islamic State? While each of the main opposition groups go to great lengths to insists that they are not actively cooperating with one another and that they are not coordinating military operations in any way, the fact remains they are all fighting a common enemy. Moreover, while each side denies that they are coordinating military operations, it is likely that some base level of communications, "back door" or otherwise, is occurring between at least some of the usually mutually antagonistic parties. The complexity of the current situation in Syria and Iraq underscores the point that we are still in the first act of what will be an exceedingly long and complex drama. The enemy of my enemy may not yet be my friend, indeed it may never be my friend, but it is, at least, if not less of an enemy, then no longer among my most important enemies. Such are the subtleties of contemporary Middle East politics.

Chapter 7

Islamic State: Terror as a Media Strategy

On August 19, 2014, Islamic State uploaded a short, four and a half minute video on YouTube entitled "A Message to America." The video began with a segment of US president Barack Obama announcing that the United States had begun conducting air strikes against IS forces in Iraq. The video then cut to a segment depicting American freelance journalist James Foley. Dressed in an orange tunic, vaguely similar to the tunics at times worn by detainees at the Guantanamo Bay Detention Camp, a kneeling Foley read a statement expressing regret for US actions. When Foley has finished reading his statement, a masked, black clad, IS fighter who was the executioner, denounced the air strikes and threatened that further American aggression would result "in the bloodshed of your people."

The video then showed a 10-second segment purporting to be the beheading of James Foley. The actual decapitation is not shown. It has been suggested that the film doesn't actually show Foley being beheaded and that the act of decapitation occurred off film. The video then shows the decapitated body while the executioner announced that IS was also holding a second American journalist, *Time Magazine* contributor, Steven Joel Sotloff, and that he would be executed if the White House did not suspend further air strikes against IS. On September 2, 2014, a second video, this one showing the beheading of Sotloff, was released. This was the beginning of a long succession of beheadings that culminated with the executions of Japanese hostages Haruna Yukawa and Kenji Goto in January 2015.

A few days later, on February 3, 2015, in an even more grisly escalation of its repertoire of murder, Islamic State militants released a video showing Jordanian Air Force pilot, Lieutenant Muath al-Kaseasbeh, being burned to death while imprisoned in a metal cage. The slickly produced, 22-minute video, titled "Healing of the Believers' Chests," showed the pilot standing in the cage with a fuel line leading to him. It also appears that his orange tunic, seemingly identical to the one that James Foley had been made to wear, had been doused with fuel. When the fuel was ignited Lieutenant Kaseasbeh caught fire and burned to death.

These acts of murder occurred against a backdrop of widespread violence, including summary execution, crucifixion, forced conversions to Islam, death by immolation and sexual slavery, instigated by IS militants across its recently seized territory in Syria and Iraq.[133] The murders were quickly denounced throughout the world as acts of unspeakable barbarism and were equally condemned by a number of Islamic groups. This was not the first time, however, that beheadings or immolations had been used as an instrument of strategy by radical Islamist organizations. Moreover, their recent use by such groups notwithstanding, neither the act of beheading or immolation, is a particularly or uniquely Islamist practice.

The Origins of Beheadings as Capital Punishment

Beheading or decapitation is a practice that dates back deep into the recesses of antiquity.[134] Its root is the Latin word *caput* or head. It is the root of such terms as "capital punishment," "capital crimes," or "capital offense." It was the punishment meted out for particularly serious crimes. In times of war it was the means by which a victor demonstrated his absolute triumph over an opponent. David, after stunning Goliath with a stone from his sling, proceeded to cut off his head with Goliath's own sword. In Greek mythology Perseus decapitated the head of Medusa and then used her head as a weapon against his enemies. Decapitation, as a punishment, was widespread from Roman times, where it was considered preferable to crucifixion, through the Middle Ages and to the modern era. From Cicero to Anne Boleyn to Robespierre, beheading was often the punishment handed down to those deemed to be enemies of the state.

The guillotine, a mechanical form of decapitation deemed to be more humane, was the only legal method of execution in France from 1789 until 1981; when capital punishment was abolished. A German version, a guillotine like device called a "falling axe" or *fallbeil* was used in Germany from the seventeenth through the twentieth centuries. Between 1933 and 1945, approximately 16,500 people were guillotined in Nazi Germany. West Germany abolished the practice in 1949. East Germany abolished it in 1966 after the execution of Horst Fischer, a former "doctor" at the Auschwitz concentration camp. Similar instruments, including precursors to the guillotine, were used throughout continental Europe and Great Britain between the twelfth and twentieth centuries. The same practice of beheading as a form of capital punishment was also widespread in Asia. Interestingly enough, beheadings as a form of capital punishment was never widespread in North American and the practice quickly died out.

Beheadings and Jihadists

Beheadings are still a legal form of punishment in Saudi Arabia, Iran, Qatar, and Yemen, although only Saudi Arabia still carries out such executions. In 2014, Saudi authorities executed 83 people, approximately half of who were foreigners.[135] Radical Islamist groups point to both Mohammed and the Koran as justification of beheadings. According to Islamic lore, Mohammed ordered the beheading of Nadr ibn al-Harith and Uqbah ibn Abu Mu'ayt, two pagan opponents of Islam captured at the Battle of Badr. The ninth century Arab historian al-Waqidi claimed that Mohammed ordered the beheading of some 900 men of the Banu Qurayza tribe, although later Arab historians have disputed the account as unreliable. The 47th Surah of the Koran, often cited by Islamist radicals, states, according to the translation by historian Timothy Furnish, that "when you encounter the unbelievers on the battlefield strike off their heads until you have crushed them completely."[136]

The first reported case of a beheading by radical Islamist groups date back to the war in Bosnia and Herzegovina (1992-95). There were a number of beheadings of Serb and Croat soldiers who had been captured by mujahedeen members of the Bosnian Army. Approximately 30 Serb civilians were also beheaded on Trebevic Mountain above Sarajevo and their bodies buried at the mass grave at Kazani. The International Criminal Tribunal for the former Yugoslavia (ICTY) documented both incidents in its investigation of war crimes committed during the Bosnian war.[137] There were reports of numerous other beheadings that were investigated but not pursued by the ICTY for lack of evidence.

The second reported incident of beheadings occurred during the First Chechen War (1994-96). On May 23, 1996, Chechens beheaded Yevgeny Rodionov, a Russian soldier, for refusing to renounce his religion and convert to Islam. A second Russian soldier, Andrey Trusov, met the same fate. Rodionov has become widely venerated as a martyr by Russian Orthodox Christians, although the Russian church has not officially recognized him as such.[138]

The first beheading to generate widespread public attention was the murder of American journalist Daniel Pearl on February 1, 2002. A militant group called the National Movement for the Restoration of Pakistani Sovereignty kidnapped Pearl, the South Asia Bureau Chief of the *Wall Street Journal*, on January 23, 2002. The group sent an email message to the US government claiming that Pearl was a spy. They demanded, among other things, the immediate freeing of all Pakistani detainees held by the

US military and the release of a suspended shipment of F-16 fighter planes to Pakistan.[139] In what was to become a familiar pattern, on February 21, 2002, a videotape titled "The Slaughter of the Spy-Journalist, the Jew Daniel Pearl," was released. The video lasted three minutes and thirty-six seconds and showed Pearl reading a statement denouncing American foreign policy. Following the statement, his throat was slit and his head was severed.

On March 21, 2002, four men were charged with the kidnapping and murder of Daniel Pearl. They were convicted on July 15, 2002, and their leader Ahmed Omar Saeed Sheikh was sentenced to death. Omar Saeed Sheikh has repeatedly appealed his sentence but hearings on the matter have been repeatedly postponed. All four men remain in prison. London born and raised, Omar Saeed Sheikh had ties to the Pakistani Directorate for Inter-Services Intelligence (ISI), but the nature and extent of these ties has never been fully disclosed. On March 10, 2007, Khalid Sheikh Mohammed, widely considered to have been the third in command of al-Qaeda and the architect of numerous terrorist attacks, including the one on September 11, during a hearing of the Combatant Status Review Tribunal held at the detention facility at Guantanamo Bay, claimed responsibility for the murder of Daniel Pearl.[140] Subsequent FBI analysis of the original video confirmed that the hand that held the knife that killed Daniel Pearl was virtually identical to that of Khalid Sheikh Mohammed.[141] The actual relationship between al-Qaeda and the original group that kidnapped Pearl remains unclear, although the four men originally charged with the murder claimed they were acting under orders of Khalid.

On March 19, 2003, an "international" force consisting primarily of combat troops from the United States (148,000) and Great Britain (45,000), with token amounts from Australia and Poland, began an invasion of Iraq. Dubbed, "Operation Iraqi Freedom," major combat operations lasted just 21 days. Almost immediately, insurgent activity began in the Sunni heartland of Iraq. A group calling itself Jam'at al-Tawhid wal-Jihad (Organization of Monotheism and Jihad or Tawhid and Jihad) previously organized by Abu Musab al-Zarqawi took a leading role in the insurgency. Tawhid and Jihad, would undergo various name changes over the following twelve years and would eventually morph into the Islamic State (IS). Between 2003 and 2006, a total of approximately 200 foreign nationals and thousands of Iraqis were kidnapped by various groups of Islamic militants. Some of the hostages were subsequently released or liberated by coalition forces. Some were murdered, although not beheaded. Some hostages were never recovered and the manner of their deaths or remains are still unknown.

The first American beheaded during the Iraqi insurgency was Nicholas Berg, murdered on May 7, 2004 by al-Zarqawi. In a video released on the website of Muntada al-Ansar, "Helpers Forum," the jihadists claimed that the murder was in retaliation for abuses at Abu Ghraib. Over the course of 2004, Tawhid and Jihad would take responsibility for seven more beheadings of foreigners.

Kim Sun Il, a South Korean citizen, was beheaded on June 22, 2004, Georgi Lazov and Ivalio Kepov, two Bulgarian citizen were beheaded in July 2004. Lazov's body was found on July 14 and Kepov's body was found on July 22. Mohammed Mutawalli, an Egyptian citizen, was beheaded on August 10, 2004. There were twelve Nepalese taken hostage on August 23, 2004. A video from August 31, 2004, showed the beheading of one and the shooting in the head of the eleven others.

Eugene Armstrong and Jack Hensley, both US citizens, and Kenneth Bigley, a British citizen, were kidnapped on September 16, 2004. Al-Zarqawi then issued a communiqué demanding the release of all female prisoners held at the Abu Ghraib prison. Armstrong was beheaded on September 20 and Hensley was beheaded on September 21. Bigley was beheaded sometime in October 2004. In addition Shosei Koda, a Japanese citizen, was beheaded by on October 30, 2004, by Tawhid and Jihad jihadists operating under their new name "al-Qaeda in Iraq." Instances of beheadings against foreign nationals diminished after 2006. Although such actions against Iraqi citizens continued, but were generally unreported in the Western media.

The emergence of ISIS during 2013 brought a resurgence of the use of beheadings as an instrument of terror. Unconfirmed reports of beheadings of Syrian troops began in the spring of 2012, shortly after the arrival of radical jihadists in the Syrian Civil War. Beginning in 2013, however, and accelerating in 2014, reports of retaliatory beheadings carried out by jihadists began to increase.[142] The first concrete evidence of beheadings by ISIS jihadists occurred on July 25, 2014, when a video was posted on social media showing the murder of approximately 75 Syrian Army soldiers from a recently captured base.

Since August 2014, a total of eight people, three Americans, two British, and two Japanese have been beheaded. Seven, James Foley (August 19, 2014), Steven Sotloff (September 2, 2014), David Haines (September 13, 2014), Alan Henning (October 3, 2014), Peter Kassig (November 16, 2014), Haruna Yukawa (January 24, 2015) and Kenji Goto (January 31, 2015) were beheaded by IS and one, Herve Gourdel (September 24, 2014), a French citizen, was beheaded by an IS affiliate in Algeria.

On January 20, 2015, Islamic State released a video showing the two Japanese hostages, Kenji Goto and Haruna Yukawa, in its custody and threatened to kill them unless the Japanese government agreed to pay a ransom of two hundred million dollars for their release. Yukawa was subsequently beheaded by Islamic State. Baghdadi then demanded to exchange the remaining hostage, Kenji Goto, for Sajida al-Rishawi, one of the bombers of the 2005 Radisson hotel bombing in Amman. She is the sister of Mubarak al-Rishawi, a key figure in AQI, and considered Zarqawi's right hand man before he was killed. Goto was also subsequently beheaded. IS then offered to exchange Lt. Kaseasbeh for al-Rishawi. After the murder of Kaseasbeh, the Jordanian government subsequently carried out the death sentence that had previously been placed on al-Rishawi.

There are at least two Lebanese Army personnel captured by IS, or its predecessor during military operations in Syria, who have also been beheaded. There is also an unspecified number of Lebanese Army troops currently being held by IS in Syria. In addition, there is evidence that at least 125 Syrian, Kurdish, and Iraqi troops, as well as Iraqi and Syrian citizens, have been beheaded by IS militants as of the end of December 2014. The actual number is probably much higher.

Death by Immolation

Death by burning or by the application of extreme heat has an equally long history as a form of capital punishment. Typically this took the form of being burned while tied to a stake. During the Spanish Inquisition, the burning of heretics at the stake was the final act of a long complex Inquisition process; a practice called auto-da-fe. The first reference to burning as a punishment dates back to the, eighteenth century BC, code of the Babylonian King Hammurabi. It was a common practice in classical antiquity, being practiced in Egypt, and throughout the Middle East. It was a common form of execution for Christian martyrs during Roman times. In AD 326, Constantine the Great decreed burning as the punishment for men that committed rape.

During the Middle Ages it was the punishment meted out to heretics and those considered enemies of the state. Jan Hus, accused of heresy, was burned at the stake. So was John Wycliffe, though in that case he had already been dead thirty years and it was only his remains that were actually burned. The Florentine Dominican friar, Savonarola, Jacques de Molay, the head of the Knights Templar, and Joan of Arc were all burned at the stake. Burning was the preferred method for executing those judged witches and sorcerers. It's hard to know how many people have been killed by burning. Estimates for the Spanish Inquisition have ranged from as little as three thousand to as many as two hundred thousand. Likewise, the number of witches burned at the stake may have ranged from a few hundred to several hundred thousand. The last official execution by burning occurred in 1813, although there may have been unreported cases as late as 1835.

There are a few cases of death by burning in the Muslim world, but these were relatively isolated. Death by burning was often the punishment for apostates that had taken up arms against Muslim rulers. The punishment was first used during the Ridda Wars, the so-called Wars of Apostasy in AD 632 and AD 633. These were a series of military campaigns by Muhammad's successor, Abu Bakr, against certain Arabian tribes that had abandoned Islam. The practice appears from time to time as punishment for non-Muslims who had illegally entered mosques or whom had refused to convert. On the whole it was a rare practice, however. The video released by Islamic State cited an obscure Koranic verse that justified punishing those who had inflicted harm with the same means that they had used. Muslim religious scholars were quick to point out, however, that the Koran forbids the desecration of corpses by burning, and specifically condemns death by burning.

Postscript: Terror as a Media Strategy

The practice of beheading, either as murder or as capital punishment, is not a particularly Islamic tradition, its persistence in Saudi Arabia notwithstanding. Neither is the practice of murder by burning. Both practices, however, have been widely adopted among radical jihadist groups to achieve a number of different purposes.

First, it is one element of a broader pattern on violence designed to intimidate the local population in the areas controlled by IS. Like most radical revolutions, IS has sought to liquidate any potential opposition and has defined such opposition, both as anyone who has opposed it, as well as anyone who had even the remotest links with the previous governing authorities. From candidates for political office to local government administrators to community leaders, anyone who cooperated or was part of the previous government is seen as an enemy. IS can't kill everyone who worked for the previous government. It could not administer its conquered territories if it did, but it can kill enough people to persuade the rest to cooperate. It's not clear how IS decides whether it will behead an opponent or simply shoot them or resort to some other method from its extensive repertoire of murder. It does appear that particularly fierce resistance to Islamic State is often met with beheadings of captured opponents. Knowing that surrendering is likely to end with death, possibly by being beheaded or crucifixion, might spur soldiers to fight more resolutely. It might also persuade them to throw down their weapons and run away. The latter response proved to be particularly popular in the Iraqi Army during the summer and fall of 2014.

Secondly, the threat of beheading prisoners is used as a means of extortion. Although both the British and American governments have resolutely refused to pay ransoms in exchange for their nationals, other countries have quietly paid such ransoms. In addition, Iraqi and Syrian citizens have also been extorted in this way. It is estimated that IS has obtained over 100 million dollars through such ransoms and it is likely that the number is much higher.

Thirdly, beheadings allow IS to shape and control its media exposure in the West and is used as an instrument to mold the debate in the United States and Europe. Death by beheading is virtually instantaneous. It may not be much different than death by firing squad, but it is a particularly gruesome way to die. A beheading, accompanied by the requisite short video, is guaranteed to generate press coverage in the international media. It is likely that the videos of beheadings circulated by IS are edited to maximize their shock value while ensuring that they are not so revolting that they will not be watched on social media sites. The press coverage and the accompanying public reaction ensures that IS, or whichever jihadist group that committed the beheading, is portrayed as a "deadly threat" to the West and ensures that it is seen in the Islamic world as the leading edge of the jihadist struggle. Death by immolation raises the horror factor one notch higher.

Moreover, beheadings put Western governments under tremendous public pressure to "do something." The more IS threatens to behead Western hostages if the air attacks continue, the more likely it is that Western governments will continue them. Moreover, the more likely it is that Muslim communities will be viewed with suspicion and be singled out by police and security forces. There are echoes of al-Qaeda's core strategy here, namely that terrorist attacks against the West will produce an overwhelming over reaction that will serve to galvanize Islamic support for the jihadist movement. IS, in all probability, lacks the ability to engage in a spectacular 9/11 type attack against the United States. Its capabilities in Western Europe, on the other hand, are more extensive. Moreover, its capabilities notwithstanding, recent attacks in Sydney, Australia (December 15-16, 2014) and the Paris office of the satirical weekly *Charlie Hebdo* (January 7, 2015) demonstrate that Islamic State inspired, "lone wolf jihadists" can carry out terrorist attacks without the direct assistance or organization of IS. We have become so sensitive to jihadist violence against the West, that beheadings of Westerners are sufficient to galvanize a government response. In that sense such beheadings represent an act of terrorism, not just against the hostage murdered, but against Western societies in general, and ensures that the jihadist struggle is defined as an Islamic struggle against Western civilization and not just an internal conflict within Islam. The burning of Lieutenant Kasasbeh may indicate that Islamic State is ratcheting up the shock value of its executions to ensure Western audiences don't become desensitized to them.

Finally, portraying the jihadist struggle as a conflict with the West, and the accompanying media coverage it generates, acts as a powerful tool for recruitment and fund raising. While support from wealthy donors now represents only a small portion of Islamic State's funding, it wants to hang on to that support and more importantly ensure that those funds don't go to potential jihadist rivals. A significant portion of IS's military force is made up of foreign nationals and it is estimated that it could include several thousand Westerners, mostly European, who have joined IS. The emergence of what sociologists are calling "jihadi cool," the romanticization of jihadist activity among marginalized, disillusioned Islamic youth in European cities, coupled with the prospect of a salary, has proven to be a powerful attractant. The use of Western spokesmen on beheading videos not only ensures that the message is clearly understood, but drives home the threat by underscoring that the executioner portrayed in the video might have been a neighbor or a fellow passenger on the local metro just a few months before.

As long as the beheadings of Western hostages continue to generate widespread media coverage, and powerful public reaction, they will continue as part of the tactics used by IS and other jihadist groups to try to shape Western public opinion and their governments' response. In the meantime, the "horror factor" of jihadist violence against western hostages will, in all probability, continue to increase.

Chapter 8

The Future of Islamic State

As 2015 began, Islamic State, despite some setbacks in Kobani, Syria, and elsewhere in Iraq, seemed firmly in control of the territory it had carved out in eastern Syria and western Iraq. Reports of its attempt to recruit and organize cells in Lebanon, Afghanistan, and Pakistan as well as existing affiliations in Egypt, Libya and Algeria, clearly underscored its global ambitions as well as its aim to wrest away the leadership of the international jihad movement from al-Qaeda. It's likely that similar attempts to organize IS cells, are also occurring elsewhere. The attack on the offices of the French satirical newspaper *Charlie Hebdo*, and the related attack on the Hyper Cacher supermarket in Paris, had produced the spectacle of rival jihadist organizations both claiming credit, or at the very least, a major role in the same operation. While it was not unusual for more than one organization to take credit for an attack, this usually occurred on smaller operations and typically among less well-known militant groups. This was the first instance of a high profile attack on a target in the West where two very prominent, rival organizations each claimed their involvement.

Moreover, it is likely that we have seen just the beginning of IS inspired terrorist activity in Europe. On January 15 and 16, Belgian police conducted a series of raids against a suspected IS cell in the city of Verviers. Two suspected jihadists were killed in the raid. An additional thirteen people were arrested as a result of twelve police raids in Brussels and across Belgium. The cell had been uncovered as a result of a police investigation into links between a Belgian arms dealer, Neetin Karasular, and Amedy Coulibaly, the terrorist that attacked the Hyper Cacher store in Paris. In unrelated operations, twelve more arrests were made in Paris of people believed to be linked to the attack on the office of *Charlie Hebdo*. In addition, German police arrested two suspected jihadists in a raid in Berlin. On January 16, *CNN*, citing unnamed intelligence sources, claimed that police believed there could be at least 20 separate IS cells operating in Europe, with between 120 and 180 militants. It is estimated that already, upward of 3,000 Europeans, mostly of Arab descent, have fought in the Syrian Civil War for a variety of jihadist organizations.

The raids occurred amidst mounting concern among intelligence officials that having had any further territorial expansion stymied and facing a coordinated counterattack by anti-IS forces in Syria and Iraq, Islamic State would order its militants around the world to attack Western targets in retaliation. Terrorist attacks over 2014 in Sydney, Ottawa, and elsewhere, in addition to the attacks in Paris, underscore the fact that so called "lone wolf" attacks either directly aided and abetted by IS cells, or simply inspired by IS propaganda, posed a serious threat to Western countries. So far, Islamic State inspired terrorist attacks in the West lack the operational complexity of previous al-Qaeda attacks; nor have the targets been as prominent or as dramatic. On the other hand, while the scale of violence may be less, their political and psychological impact is equally significant. A pattern of smaller, random, uncoordinated terrorist attacks is, in contrast to al-Qaeda, typical of IS's strategy. Such attacks are more difficult to anticipate, generally generate less "chatter" within terrorist networks, and are more likely to fly under the radar of Western intelligence agencies.

Islamic State: Challenges and Opportunities

The Islamic State faces a considerable set of challenges. First, it is entirely land locked. It lacks control of any port facilities. This makes resupply, especially of heavy equipment, considerably more difficult. It is completely surrounded by its opponents so any kind of overland transport is also extremely difficult. Moreover, it lacks any sort of a "sponsor" that could resupply it or give it access to advanced military equipment. While small arms and munitions are readily available on the black market, the availability of any kind of advanced or heavy equipment is limited to what it can capture on the battlefield. Additionally, it has a decided disadvantage in manpower. The number of ground forces arrayed against it, outnumber its militants by a considerable margin. The lopsided victories of the 2014 summer are unlikely to be repeated against more resolute ground troops.

Secondly, it lacks any kind of air power capability. Notwithstanding reports that IS militants have captured fighter planes and attack helicopters in Syria and Iraq, and even if it can recruit trained pilots to operate them, it lacks the ability to project air power in a meaningful way. It takes more than a pilot and a plane to project air power. Against the US Air Force, the most formidable air power in the world, any sort of air attack capability that IS might try to deploy would be quickly destroyed. Nor does it have the ability to mount any kind of coordinated air defense system. Low flying planes and attack helicopters are vulnerable to ground based fire and weapons like the FIM 92 "stinger" surface-to-air missile. IS militants were able to secure a stock of "stingers" from Iraqi Army supply depots. Exactly how many they have available is unclear, but this is likely to be a diminishing resource and access to additional stocks is doubtful. Lacking any air power projection or defense capability, IS militants are vulnerable to air attacks against concentrations of their troops or heavy equipment. Moreover, the provision of close ground support to anti-IS forces, even at the risk of attack by ground fire and stinger missiles, puts IS forces at a distinct disadvantage.

Thirdly, the ability of Islamic State to actually administer the, would be, caliphate is questionable. There are mounting reports of the continued breakdown and inadequacy of public services in the territory "administered" by Islamic State. Notwithstanding estimates that IS militants captured liquid assets estimated at between 500 million and two billion dollars from its conquered territories, there are widespread reports that Islamic State is running out of money. Hundreds of millions of dollars may seem like a healthy endowment for a militant group, but for a would be government charged with administering a territory spanning 80,000 square miles and containing more than eight million people, it will likely prove to be inadequate. Moreover, being entirely surrounded by its opponents, Islamic State is effectively cut-off from any kind of international commerce. All the money in the world will do you little good if there is nothing to buy. As of the beginning of 2015, only the Jordanian-Iraq border crossing at Turaibil was still operating, but it is unclear if any significant amount of goods were flowing across the border. Iraq's western desert is extremely permeable and there are literally hundreds of "unofficial" or illegal border crossings. While such "smuggler routes" have been used by militant organizations for years to secure supplies, it is unlikely that they are sufficient to meet the needs of a country of eight million people.

Finally, in addition to being surrounded on all sides by its opponents, those territories that are within its possible operational grasp are largely inhabited by people who are unlikely to have any sympathy for Islamic State or its political and social agenda, either because they are Shia, or because they are parts of nations strongly opposed to Islamic State. The heart of Islamic State remains the Sunni Triangle of Iraq, precisely that region that was the most unsupportive of the Baghdad Government. Having largely conquered this region, IS will find that the remaining pickings will be slim.

On the other hand there are a number of factors that will work in Islamic State's favor both to reduce the speed in which it is degraded as well as to give it more maneuvering room against its opponents. First, the anti-IS alliance is, to put it charitably, a very tenuous one. At the heart of that *de facto* alliance are two countries, the United States and Iran, that have little in agreement beyond the desirability of destroying IS and ensuring that the government in Baghdad is not overrun. Their respective policies elsewhere in the Middle East are largely incompatible. It's possible that the anti-IS alliance may mark the beginning of an American-Iranian rapprochement. The longer and more difficult the struggle against IS, the more likely such an outcome will be. Conversely, a quick victory against Islamic State will make it more likely that Washington and Tehran will revert back to mutually antagonistic policies. Moreover, at some point, when the perceived threat of Islamic State is sufficiently reduced, the coalition is likely to fracture over the issue of regime change in Syria. Maintaining the Assad government in power is a core interest of Iran, one that it can be expected to support with additional aid and troops if necessary. Syria is key to Tehran's support of Hezbollah and is essential to maintain Iran's "arc of influence" in the Middle East. Iraq too, while less able to come to the defense of the Assad government, has little interest in seeing it replaced by a Sunni led government. Such a development would further embolden Iraq's own Sunni minority and make them that much more formidable an opponent to the Baghdad Government.

Moreover, there are in fact two separate alliances: an American-Arab alliance fighting Islamic State in Syria and an American-European alliance fighting Islamic State in Iraq. Neither alliance seems interested in expanding its scope of operation beyond its current area.

Secondly, notwithstanding the forces arrayed against it, it is highly unlikely that Islamic State can be destroyed. The territory under its control can be rolled back and its leadership killed. It's possible that all of its territory could be taken back and it would be reduced to just being a militant jihadist organization. Alternatively, it could find itself in a situation where its territorial control ebbs and flows, much as it did during the preceding insurgency—withdrawing when the Baghdad government projects military force and returning when that force is withdrawn. The most likely scenario is that IS retains ongoing control of one or more pockets of territory with Syria, while its control of territory in Iraq is more fluid. At the same time it continues to conduct an insurgency against the Baghdad government while continuing to participate in the Syrian civil war.

The more pertinent question is what is it going to take to roll back Islamic State's territories? The answer to this question will depend on the extent and the quality of the "boots on the ground." Air power can degrade IS forces, it can strike at their troop concentrations and heavy equipment, it can intervene in a ground war to tip the balance in favor of the anti-IS forces, but ultimately it will take ground troops to roll back Islamic State. A popular revolt among the Sunni inhabitants of IS might speed up that process, but a revolt among poorly armed Sunni militias will, if history is any guide, be met with quick and brutal repression. The issue is, whose ground force, with or without a popular revolt, will roll back Islamic State forces and their territorial holdings?

Kurdish Peshmerga forces are, with the support of US air power and additional military supplies, probably sufficient to defend the Kurdistan Regional Government and to push IS forces out of the Kurdish areas they have seized. They are most likely both incapable and unwilling to attempt a general rollback of Islamic State elsewhere in Iraq. The one exception will be Mosul. Although not technically part of the Kurdish Autonomous Region, the city has historical and cultural significance to Iraq's Kurd community. The Battle for Mosul will likely be the next major confrontation in the war with Islamic State and will pit Peshmerga and Iraqi military forces not only against IS but to some extent against each other as each of them scrambles to take control of the city before there erstwhile ally.

Ultimately, the objective of the KRG is to create an independent Kurdish state or to secure as much autonomy as possible. They will be reluctant to put Kurdish forces at risk for anything beyond that objective. The longer it takes to degrade Islamic State, the more likely it will be that the Kurdish Government will achieve greater autonomy if not actual independence. That task of rolling back IS will fall on the Iraqi Army, supported by the Shia militias and its Iranian allies. The combat record of the Iraqi Army over the summer of 2014 was less than inspiring. Over the autumn, however, with additional help from Iran and the Shia militias, and with the benefit of the US led air strikes, the Iraqi Army's resolve and combat effectiveness seemed to have improved.

Nonetheless, without a broader political compromise with Iraq's Sunni community, and without a larger Iranian military presence in Iraq, it is likely that the process of rolling back IS will be a long and protracted one. At the moment, there is little indication that the Shia led government is willing to offer Iraq's Sunni community a meaningful level of political power and participation in governing Iraq. Without a long term political solution, eliminating Islamic State does little more than set the stage for yet another Sunni insurgency, this one led by some other militant jihadist group. An expanded Iranian military presence in Iraq is also unlikely, not unless Baghdad and the Shiite government are in danger of falling.

From Tehran's perspective, its key objective is to maintain a friendly, Shiite dominated government in Baghdad, and to ensure that it has the ability to continue to assist the Assad government and keep it in power. Keeping the current governments in Syria and Iraq in power are critical to ensuring its support for Hezbollah and to maintaining its "arc of influence" across the Middle East. As long as the Baghdad government is not in danger of collapse, an ongoing instability, if not an outright insurgency in Iraq's Sunni Triangle, does not pose a risk to Tehran's core interests. In fact, such an outcome will simply increase Baghdad's dependence on its Iranian patrons. Iran's leaders are assuming here that the deployment of ground troops from the United States or any of its Arab or European allies to Iraq is highly unlikely. So far that assumption has been correct and there is little reason to think it will not continue to be so.

Regardless of what happens to Islamic State in the future, two things are clear. First, it is rapidly expanding its reach to become the center of an international jihadist movement and, in the process, the leading edge of global jihadism. There are numerous reports of its attempts to organize IS cells in Afghanistan and Pakistan. It has active cells throughout Western Europe and is no doubt looking to expand its network there. Its predecessor organizations have long been active in Jordan, Lebanon, and elsewhere in the Middle East. In expanding its reach it is also challenging al-Qaeda for the leadership of the global jihadist movement. For the first time since 9/11 there are two, mutually antagonistic international jihadism organizations competing for the heart and mind of international jihadism. That competition will, in part, take the form of demonstrating which organization is more effective in striking out at the West. Recent terrorist attacks in Australia, Canada, France, and elsewhere, are likely to be a template for an escalating pattern of random, smaller, but widespread, lone wolf, terrorist attacks. A pattern of violence that falls somewhere in the middle of a full-scale insurgency and the "spectacular" al-Qaeda style terrorist attack.

Secondly, IS's successes to date have been sufficient to make it a permanent fixture of jihadist mythology. Regardless of its survival, its videos, Baghdadi's sermons, its history, will continue to inspire jihadists and terrorist attacks. In this sense, its evolution may well follow the path of al-Qaeda since the 9/11 attacks. Al-Qaeda has seen its ranks decimated, its charismatic leader Osama bin Laden killed, its funding networks disrupted, and many of its safe havens destroyed, yet the organization continues to exist. While it may no longer possess the capability of executing the sort of dramatic, complicated attack that it did on 9/11, it continues to inspire jihadists. By working through proxy organizations, and by granting them the mantle of its franchise, it has maintained its relevancy and jihadist credentials. Initially, that proxy organization was Zarqawi's Tawhid, the foundation of IS, which it transformed into al-Qaeda in Iraq. For the last several years, it has been al-Qaeda in the Arabian Peninsula (AQAP). That organization took responsibility for the Paris attacks, claiming that the attack had been planned by its now deceased leader Anwar al-Awlaki and had been years in the making, and has been implicated in scores of attacks against Western targets. Islamic State already has affiliates in Algeria, Libya, and Sinai, and, in keeping with the al-Qaeda model, even if it is destroyed or degraded to the point of irrelevancy, it is likely that some other "Islamic State" elsewhere will claim the IS franchise and its legacy. The success of AQAP in continuing to use al-Awlaki's videos and sermons to inspire new recruits and jihadist violence, years after his death, underscores the power of Jihadist mythology.

As of February 2015, it would seem reasonable to conclude that the territorial expansion of Islamic State has probably been effectively stopped. It is likely that its boundaries will be rolled back but that this will be a slow and protracted process. The air power of the United States and its various allies will be sufficient to degrade IS's capabilities but probably insufficient to lead to its widespread collapse, much less its destruction. Combined with other pressures, however, it may be sufficient to force it to revert back into a widespread urban insurgency. The issue of regime change in Syria remains unresolved as does the broader Shia-Sunni/Iran-Saudi Arabia and Turkish competition for influence in the Middle East, and these two issues will fracture the anti-Islamic State alliance. How the struggle against IS and the ongoing war in Syria will ultimately affect American-Iranian relations and their relevancy on US attempts to control Iran's nuclear development program also remain to be seen. In the short term, pressure on IS from its opponents, as well as its competition with al-Qaeda, will likely mean an expansion of low level, lone wolf terrorist attacks against the West. The struggle against Islamic State and the consequences of its rise are just beginning. An already incredibly complex political situation in the Middle East is likely to grow even more complex. What is manifestly clear is that there are no easy answers.

JVM February 5, 2015

Acknowledgements

Thanks are owed to several people. Carla Micallef has been,
as always, a consummate editor and assistant. Eric Garland was a
consummate designer. Finally to the many friends, acquaintances
and contacts in the Middle East, and especially in Iraq and Syria, who
made innumerable contributions to this book and whose identities,
for their own safety, will have to remain confidential for now.

Footnotes

1. In tracing the evolution of Islamic State I have used the name it adopted during the particular historic period being covered. Hence, Tawhid, AQI, ISI, ISIS and IS all denote the same organization at different periods of its evolution. ISIS and ISIL are both correct, depending whether one uses the Arabic word for the Levant, (al Sham) for the final "S" or the "L" from the English translation of "al Sham" into Levant. The "S" in ISIS has never stood for the term "Syria." I have used the designation ISIS in preference to ISIL. The idea of "Syria," both as a nation and as a region, is a Western concept that dates back to antiquity and had no political significance under either Arab or Ottoman administrations.

2. There are numerous, excellent articles on Zarqawi's background. See, in particular "Profile: Abu Musab al-Zarqawi", *BBC News*. November 10, 2005. Smith, Laura "Timeline Abu Musab al-Zarqawi", *The Guardian*, June 8, 2006. "Profile: of Abu Musab al-Zarqawi", *Global Security*, June 8, 2006. Whitlock, Craig "Al-Zarqawi's Biography", *Washington Post*, June 8, 2006. This summary of Zarqawi's background is drawn from a variety of public sources as well as a number of private communications.

3. McCanta, William, Editor and Project Coordinator, *Militant Ideology Atlas*, Combating Terrorism Center, U.S. Military Academy, 2006.

4. Private communication. See also the comments by Bergen, Peter *The Osama bin Laden I Know*, Free Press, 2006, P. 359-422.

5. Brisard, Jean Charles and Martinez, Damien *Zarqawi: The New Face of Al Qaeda*, Other Press, July 17, 2005 has useful information but is poorly written.

6. There are conflicting versions of this story. Some accounts claim the extradition request was made to the Iranian government while other versions claim it was to the Iraqi government of Saddam Hussein.

7. Hayes, Stephen: "What Zarqawi–and al-Qaeda–were up to before the Iraq war," *The Weekly Standard*, June 19, 2006. Hayes, Stephen: "What Zarqawi–and al-Qaeda–were up to before the Iraq war," *The Weekly Standard*, June 19, 2006.

8. "Zarqawi set up Iraq sleeper cells: UK report", *Associated Press*, July 15, 2004.
9. Claims by militant organizations, or for that matter by US officials, were often reported verbatim by Western media with little if any attempt at independent verification. Truthfully, many of the claims could not have been verified anyway. What attempts at verification occurred usually were little more than finding another source to parrot back the same claim. See for example, Miklaszewski, Jim "With Tuesday's Attack, Abu Musab Zarqawi is now blamed for more than 700 terrorist killings in Iraq", *NBC News*, March 2, 2004. This claim was widely carried by the Western media but it was never independently verified.
10. See "Fedayeen Enforces Loyalty Among Iraqi Army", *Washington Post*, March 24, 2003 and "What is the Fedayeen Saddam," *New York Times*, (From a report by the Council on Foreign Relations), March 25, 2003.
11. Private communication.
12. The bombing was originally blamed on Ba'athist militants. Saddam Hussein subsequently released an audiotape denying any Bath Party involvement in the attack. Zarqawi praised the bomber on the Tawhid website and in various audiotapes. He never specifically identified the bomber, however, and it is unclear where the reference to his father-in-law came from.
13. The quotation is drawn from a lengthy letter that Zarqawi addressed to the Sunni community in Iraq. See "Al-Zarqawi's Message," April 6, 2004 fas.org. See also an earlier letter from Zarqawi echoing many of the same thoughts that was released in February 2004. U.S. Department of State Archives, 2001-2009.state.gov.
14. Whitlock, Craig "Al-Zarqawi's Biography," *Washington Post*, June 8 2006. The source of the chemical cache has never been discovered. Small quantities of chemicals were frequently discovered at safe houses frequented by Zarqawi. He had a long-standing reputation of being knowledgeable about the use of chemical weapons and of being partial to them however, it does not appear that he ever used any during the Iraqi insurgency. It has been suggested that those chemical agents originated in pre-Iraqi war, Ba'ath sources, however no concrete evidence of any such links has ever emerged. The ultimate source of those chemicals remains a mystery.

15. U.S. Intelligence agencies had tried to establish a direct link between Zarqawi and bin Laden, typically citing their past contact in Afghanistan and financial support that Zarqawi had received from al Qaeda in the past. Intelligence reports, declassified by the Bush administration in 2007, claimed that Zarqawi had been dispatched to Iraq specifically on bin Laden's orders to organize an insurgency and attack American troops. In addition, over the course of 2004, U.S. intelligence agencies obtained copies of various letters from Ayman al-Zawahiri advising Zarqawi on strategy and tactics and, in one instance, warning him that his attacks on Iraqi Shias would turn Muslim public opinion against him. See, for example, Silva, Mark "Bush declassifies selected Al Qaeda intelligence reports," Chicago Tribune, May 23, 2007. In reality it is more likely that although Zarqawi availed himself of any assistance that al Qaeda could render, he operated largely independent of it, and had significant differences with al Qaeda's leadership. Zawahiri's letters were probably an attempt of al-Qaeda's leadership to assert a more prominent role in the Iraqi insurgency rather than an example of issuing orders to a subordinate. See also the report of the U.S. Senate Select Committee on Intelligence, *Postwar Findings About Iraq's WMD Program*, GPO: Washington DC, September 8, 2006 at intelligence. senate.gov.

16. See Devin, Springer: *Islamic Radicalism and Global Jihad*, Georgetown University Press, 2009.

17. See McGrath, Kevin: *Confronting Al Qaeda: New Strategies to Combat Terrorism*, Naval Institute Press, 2011 , especially pg. 116.

18. The text of Zarqawi's comments is reprinted in "The Fourth State of the Iraq Jihad" at kavkazcenter.com.

19. "Al-Khalayleh tribe disowns al-Zarqawi", *Jerusalem Post*, November 20, 2005.

20. The letter was posted on the web site of the Director of National Intelligence John D Negroponte at: http://www.dni.gov/. See also "Letter from al-Zawahiri to al-Zarqawi" in globalsecurity.org.

21. See Mujahedeen Shura Council (Iraq) at itec-sde.net.

22. Kennicot, Phillip: "A Chilling Portrait Unsuitably Framed," *Washington Post*, June 12, 2006.

23. Private communication.

24. Robertson, Campbell: "Terrorist or Mythic Symbol: A Tale of Iraqi Politics," *New York Times*, May 30, 2009.
25. Islamic State even went so far as to issue an "Annual Report" of its activities complete with pie charts and graphs illustrating its activities and acts of terrorism. See footnote #127 for additional details.
26. "Pressure Grows in al Qaeda in Iraq," *ABC News*, February 4, 2006.
27. See the brief on the Mujahedeen Shura Council (MSC), at terrorism.com.
28. Gordon, Michael: "Leader of Al-Qaeda in Iraq was fictional, U.S. military says," *New York Times*, July 18, 2007.
29. Serrano, Alfonso: "U.S.: Key Al-Qaeda in Iraq Figure Caught," *CBS News*, July 18, 2007.
30. Timmerman, Kenneth: *Shadow Warriors: The Untold Story of Traitors, Saboteurs, and the Party of Surrender*, Three Rivers Press, 2008 has a rather convoluted and at times controversial account of CIA activity in Iraq in the period before and immediately following the 2003 invasion. While plausible, much of it is unsubstantiated.
31. Parker, Ned: "Abu Abed: Ruthless, Shadowy, and a U.S. Ally in Iraq," the *LA Times*, December 27, 2007.
32. Ricks, Thomas E.: "Situation Called Dire in Western Iraq," *Washington Post*, September 11, 2006.
33. "US buys 'concerned citizens' in Iraq, but at what price?" *Associated Press*, October 16, 2007.
34. See Katzman, Kenneth: "Iraq: Politics, Governance and Human Rights," *Congressional Research Service*, October 29, 2014. See also, "Iraq's Sunnis Fear Life Without US Oversight," *ABC News* October 1, 2008.
35. See Izady, Michael: "Ethnic Cleansing in Baghdad" at brusselstribunal.org. See also the commentary at Musings on Iraq, "Columbia University Charts Sectarian Cleansing of Baghdad," musingsoniraq.blogspot.com.
36. Friedman, Thomas: *From Beirut to Jerusalem*, New York: Farrar Straus and Giroux, 2010.
37. "Syrian Opposition Alliance," *BBC News*, November 16, 2011.
38. The day-to-day conflict in Syria has been extensively covered by the international news media. I have therefore not cited specific references in the summary of the conflict. Among the better sources of daily, ongoing coverage, are the *BBC News* "Syria's War," *Al Monitor* "Syrian Pulse," and *Al Jazeera* "Syria." *The*

Guardian, The New York Times and *The Daily Telegraph*, have also have ongoing, in-depth coverage of the Syrian Civil War. I have continued, however, to cite references for particularly important and controversial points. See also the detailed summary by Holliday, Joseph "Syria's Armed Opposition" *Middle East Security Report 3*, Institute for the Study of War, March 2012.

39. "Islamist group claims Syria bombs 'to avenge Sunnis,'" *Al Arabiya*, (English edition), March 21, 2012.
40. Echoing, Zarqawi's tactics, al-Nusra boasted on its website that it was responsible for the bulk of the suicide bombings in Syria.
41. "Syrians decry US blacklisting of rebel group," *Al Jazeera*, December 15, 2012.
42. Sherlock, Ruth: "Inside Jabhat al Nusra," *The Telegraph* December 2, 2012.
43. "Qaeda in Iraq Confirms Syria's Nusra is Part of Network," *Agence France-Presse*, April 9, 2013.
44. "Al-Nusra Commits to al-Qaeda, Deny Iraq Branch "Merger," *Agence France Presse*, April 10, 2013.
45. "Qaeda Chief Annuls Syrian-Iraqi Jihad Merger," *Al Jazeera* June 9, 2013.
46. "Iraqi al-Qaeda Chief Rejects Zawahiri's Order," *Al Jazeera* June 15, 2013.
47. Sly, Liz: "Al Qaeda Disavows Any Ties with Radical Islamist Group in Syria and Iraq," *The Washington Post*, February 3, 2014.
48. "Syria: al-Nusra Front Declares War on ISIS," *al-Akhbar* (English edition) February 26, 2014.
49. Zavadski, Katie: "ISIS now Has a Network of Military Affiliates in 11 Countries Around the World," *New York Magazine*, November 23, 2014.
50. Navon, Emmanuel: "Iran, Hezbollah assisting in Syria protest suppression," *Jerusalem Post* March 27, 2011.
51. Tisdall, Simon: "Iran helping Syrian Regime crack down on protestors, say diplomats," *The Guardian* May 9, 2011.
52. "How Iran Keeps Assad in Power in Syria," *Inside Iran*, September 5, 2011.
53. "Syrian Army being aided by Iranian forces," *The Guardian*, May 28, 2012.
54. "Iran supplying Syrian Military via Iraqi Airspace," *New York Times*, Sept 4, 2012.

55. Charbonneau, Louis: "Exclusive: Iran Flouts U.N. sanctions, sends arms to Syria," *Reuters*, May 16, 2012.
56. "Iran accused of setting up pro-Assad militias," *Al Jazeera*, August 15, 2012.
57. Walsh, Nick Patton: "Iranian drones guiding Syrian attacks, rebels say," *CNN* October 31, 2012.
58. Fisk, Robert "Iran to send 4,000 troops to aid President Assad forces in Syria," *The Independent*, June 16, 2013.
59. Sherlock, Ruth: "Iran boosts support to Syria," *The Telegraph*, February 21, 2014.
60. Holliday, Joseph: "Syria's Armed Opposition," *Middle East Security Report 3*, Institute for the Study of War, March 2012.
61. "Iran bolsters military support to Syria," *Reuters*, February 21, 2014.
62. "Syrian Crisis: The Long road to Damascus," *The Economist*, February 11, 2012.
63. Private communication.
64. Nadimi, Farzim: "Iran is Expanding its Military Role in Iraq," The Washington Institute for Near Eastern Policy, September 10, 2014.
65. "Barzani: Iran supplied weapons to Peshmerga forces," *Daily Star* (Beirut), August 26, 2014.
66. See the BBC profile of Soleimani in Sharafedin, Bozorgmehr "Iran's Qasem Soleimani wields power behind the scenes in Iraq," *BBC News*, June 17, 2014. See also the ongoing coverage of Soleimani's role in Iraq in *Al Monitor*.
67. Gordon, Michael: "Iran Secretly Sending Drones and Supplies into Iraq," *New York Times*, June 25, 2014.
68. Blanford, Nicholas: "Why Hezbollah is playing a smaller role in this Iraqi conflict," *Christian Science Monitor*, July 16, 2014.
69. Jassem Al Salami: "Iran Sends Tanks to Iraq to Fight ISIS," *Real Clear Defense*, August 25, 2014.
70. "First footage surfaces: Iranian Jets seen attacking ISIS targets in Iraq," *Haaretz*, December 1, 2014.
71. "Iran Jets bomb Islamic state targets in Iraq-Pentagon," *BBC News*, December 3, 2014.
72. McCabe, David: "Iran has sent more than 1,000 military advisors to fight ISIS in Iraq," thehill.com.
73. "Russian Military Presence in Syria Poses Challenge to US-led Intervention," *The Guardian*, December 23, 2012.

74. "Russia steps up military lifeline to Syria's Assad," Reuters, January 17, 2014.
75. Russia did propose, under UN supervision, a plan for the destruction of Assad's chemical weapons arsenal, but the degree of compliance by the Syrian government to the plan is unclear. It's equally unclear what advantage the Kremlin gained from its proposal beyond that of a small public relations victory over the White House.
76. Hirst, David: "Hezbollah uses its military power in a contradictory manner," The Daily Star (Beirut), October 23, 2012.
77. Parraga, Marianna: "Venezuela to ship more fuel to Syria as crackdown spreads," Reuters, March 6, 2012.
78. "North Korean Officers Helping Syrian Government Forces," The Chosun Llbo, June 5, 2013.
79. "Behind the Lines: Assad's North Korean Connection," Jerusalem Post, November 2, 2013.
80. Roggio, Bill; "U.S. Aided Hezbollah Brigades in breaking Islamic State siege of Iraqi Town," Long War Journal, September 10, 2014.
81. Private communication.
82. "Arab League Allows members to arm rebels and offers seat to opposition," Al Bawaba, February 9, 2013.
83. Khalaf, Roula: "Qatar Bankrolls Syrian revolt with cash and arms," Financial Times, May 16, 2013.
84. Private communication.
85. "Syrian Rebels Describe U.S. backed Training in Qatar," Frontline (Public Broadcasting Service), May 26, 2014.
86. "In Shift, Saudis are Said to Arm Rebels in Syria," New York Times, February 26, 2013.
87. "Saudi Arabia replaces Intelligence Chief," The Guardian, April 15, 2014.
88. Ybarra, Maggie "U.S. is sending 400 troops to train Syrian fighters against Islamic State," Washington Times, January 16, 2015. These camps are separate from the CIA run camps in Turkey and Jordan.
89. "Syria crisis: Saudi Arabia To Spend Millions To Train New Rebel Force," The Guardian, November 7, 2013.
90. O'Bagy, Elizabeth: "Middle East Security Report: Jihad in Syria," Institute for the Study of War, Washington DC, 2012.
91. See the ongoing coverage in AL-Monitor at al-monitor.com, a daily coverage of Arabic media for the latest permutations of the ever-

shifting landscape of rebel groups and rebel coalitions in the Syrian civil war.

92. The role of Turkish intelligence (MIT) in the Syrian civil war has been a controversial one. On January 1, 2015, the Turkish newspaper *Hurriyet* broke a story that MIT was shipping weapons to al Qaeda affiliated groups in Syria. See Idiz, Semih: "Turkey Pulse" *Al Monitor*, January 3, 2014.

93. See the report, among others, at http://www.todayszaman.com/news-343357-turkish-journalist-detained-over-leak-of-key-syria-meeting.html.

94. Hosenball, Mark: "Obama authorizes secret US support for Syrian rebels," *Reuters*, August 1, 2012.

95. Schmitt, Eric: "CIA Said to Aid in Steering Arms to Syrian Opposition," *New York Times*, June 21, 2012.

96. "Remarks by the President to the White House Press Corps," whitehouse.gov, August 20, 2012.

97. Gordon, Michael R.: "Senate Hearing Draws Out Rift in US Policy on Syria," *New York Times*, February 7, 2013.

98. MacFarquhar, Neil: "With Eye of Aid, Syria Opposition Signs Unity Deal," *New York Times*, November 11, 2012.

99. Cloud, David S.: "U.S. has secretly provided arms training to Syria rebels since 2012," *Los Angeles Times*, June 21, 2013.

100. Entous, Adam: "CIA Expands Role in Syria Fight," *Wall Street Journal*, March 22, 2013.

101. Mazzetti, Mark: "Obama's Uncertain Path Amid Syria Bloodshed," *New York Times,* October 22, 2013.

102. "United States Announces Additional Humanitarian Assistance For Syrian Crisis," state.gov, June 4, 2014.

103. "EU May Provide Training to Syrian Rebels," *Spiegel*, March 4, 2013.

104. Cooper, Helene: "Obama Requests Money to Train Appropriately Vetted Syrian Rebels," *New York Times*, June 26, 2014.

105. Entous, Adam: "U.S. Secretly Flying Drones Over Iraq," *Wall Street Journal*, June 12, 2014.

106. Siegel, Jacob: "Will U.S. Troops Stand By While ISIS Starves Thousands," *The Daily Beast*, August 7, 2014.

107. Roggio, Bill: "US Airpower supports Peshmerga, Iraqi Forces to retake Mosul Dam," *The Long War Journal*, August 18, 2014.

108. Lucas, Mary Grace: "ISIS nearly made it to Baghdad airport, top U.S. military leader says," *CNN* October 13, 2014.

109. Mora, Edwin: "Pentagon: 'No Indication' U. S. Troops Engaged in Ground Combat with ISIS in Iraq," breitbart.com, December 18, 2014.

110. Hafezi, Parisa: "U.S. told Iran of intent to strike Islamic State in Syria," *Reuters*, September 23, 2014.

111. Collard, Rebecca: "Syria Informed In Advance of U.S. Led Air Strikes against Islamic State," *Washington Post*, September 23, 2014.

112. The territorial scope of Islamic State is open to question. Much of its domain is uninhabited desert. There are few roads in the region. Most of the population lives in a handful of larger cities and towns. The size of IS has been estimated to be anywhere from 12,000 to 80,000 square miles depending on how on counts the desert area of western Iraq and eastern Syria and what constitutes "control" over this region. See the ongoing updates in "Areas under ISIS Control," *New York Times*, January 2, 2015.

113. See Piven, Ben: "Iraq violence continues after US withdrawal," *Al Jazeera*, March 8, 2012. The coverage of the civil war in Iraq following the withdrawal of the last U.S. troops on December 17, 2011 has been extensively covered in the international media. See specifically the ongoing coverage by the *BBC News, Al Jazeera* as well as the coverage in *The New York Times, The Guardian*, and *The Independent*. I have not cited references in the general summary of events but I have cited references of points that were important or controversial.

114. "Iraqi crisis stirs protests in Sunni strongholds," *Jerusalem Post*, December 23, 2011.

115. Marwan, Ibrahim: "protest-related violence kills 53 in Iraq," *Associated Press*.

116. Tawfeeq, Mohammed: "Islamist group ISIS claims deadly Lebanon blast, promises more violence," *CNN*, January 4, 2014.

117. "Al-Qaeda-linked groups expand into Lebanon," *Al Jazeera*, January 26, 2014.

118. The emergence of ISIS affiliated Taliban groups was subsequently confirmed during the summer of 2014. Private communication. See also Tan, Michelle "ISIS recruiting in Afghanistan, Pakistan," *Army Times*, January 15, 2015.

119. Chulov, Martin "Syrian rebels oust al-Qaida-affiliated jihadists from northern city of Raqqa," *The Guardian* January 6, 2014.

120. Holmes, Oliver: "Al Qaeda breaks links with Syrian militant group ISIL," *Reuters* February 3, 2014.
121. "Two people arrested in connection with the attack in Istanbul," *Dogan News Agency* March 25, 2014.
122. Soffer, Ari: "Syrian Islamists Stage Public Crucifixions," *Arutz Sheva*, May 1 , 2014.
123. Jane Arraf: "Iraqi Sunni Tribal Leaders Say Fight for Fallujah is Part of a Revolution," *Washington Post*, June 15, 2014.
124. Bayoumi, Alaa, Harding, Leah: "Mapping Iraqi Fighting Groups," *Al Jazeera*, June 27, 2014.
125. See "Who's who in Iraq: Sunni Groups," *BBC News*, June 17, 2004. See also Nasr, Vali *The Shia Revival*, Norton 2006 for additional background as well as the ongoing coverage in *Al Jazeera*.
126. Strange, Hannah: "Isis Crisis," *The Telegraph*, June 13, 2014.
127. Private communication.
128. For ongoing coverage of the status of Iraqi border crossings see "Areas Under ISIS Control," *New York Times,* January 2, 2015.
129. See "Iraqi military claims victories", *CNN*, June 14, 2014. See also the coverage by Scarborough, Rowan, "Iran's Quds Force helping Iraqi Shiites with Obama's Administration's Blessings," *The Washington Times*, September 20, 2014.
130. *BBC News,* "Militants 'seize' city of Tal Afar," June 16, 2014. The executions may have been a reprisal for the execution of 255 Sunni prisoners by the Iraqi Army when it withdrew from Tal Afar. See also *Al Jazeera*, July 12, 2014.
131. According to a report in the *Washington Times,* "Peshmerga forces were aided by the Iranian Quds Force." The battle featured U.S. airpower providing close ground close support, for the first time, whether intentional or inadvertent, to Quds troops. Both sides denied that there had been any coordinated cooperation. See also footnote #122.
132. Private communication.
133. The atrocities committed by IS have been extensively documented by a variety of organizations and news organizations. See in particular the detailed report from the UN High Commissioner for Human Rights, *Report on the Protection of Civilians in Armed Conflict in Iraq: 6 July-10 September 2014*, New York: United Nations, 2014. Unbelievably, Islamic State has issued a 410 page "Annual Report," called *al-Naba*, where it documents the scope

and extent of its atrocities. The report, in Arabic, is available at azelin.files.wordpress.com. For an English language synopsis see Talaga, Tanya "Islamic State issues 'annual report' detailing atrocities," *Toronto Star* October 8, 2014.

134. See "Execution by beheading" (decapitation) at capitalpunishmentuk.org and Larson, Francis, *Severed: A History of Heads Lost and Heads Found* Liveright (W.W. Norton & Company), 2014 for a history of the practice of decapitation.
135. "Saudi beheadings spiked in 2014 amid Kingdom's fear of dissent," *Fox News*, January 5, 2014.
136. Furnish, Timothy R.: "Beheading in the Name of Islam," *Middle East Quarterly*, Spring 2005.
137. See the ongoing reports of the International Criminal Tribunal for Yugoslavia (ICTY) at icr.icty.org.
138. "Boy soldier who died for faith made 'saint,'" *The Daily Telegraph*, January 24, 2014.
139. Pellegrini: "Frank Daniel Pearl 1963-2002," *Time Magazine*, February 21, 2002.
140. "Verbatim Transcript of Combatant Status Review Tribunal Hearing for ISN 10024 (Khalid Sheik Mohammed)," US Department of Defense, March 10, 2007.
141. Ackerman, Spencer: "Qaeda Killer Veins Implicate Him in Journo's Murder," *Wired*, January 20, 2011.
142. See "Horrific video shows Syrian Catholic priest being beheaded by jihadist fighters," *Daily Mail*, July 1, 2013 and Enoch, Nick, "Beheaded in front of children, Assad's thugs are dragged to their doom," *Daily Mail* September 13, 2013. These are the first documented instances of beheadings during the Syrian Civil War and were carried out by the al-Nusra Front. It is likely that there were earlier, unreported instances, of beheadings.

www.ingramcontent.com/pod-product-compliance
Lightning Source LLC
Chambersburg PA
CBHW071608040426
42452CB00008B/1284